The old-time pamphlet ethos is back, with some of the most challenging work being done today. Prickly Paradigm Press is devoted to giving serious authors free rein to say what's right and what's wrong about their disciplines and about the world, including what's never been said before. The result is intellectuals unbound, writing unconstrained and creative texts about meaningful matters.

"Long live Prickly Paradigm Press.... Long may its flaming pamphlets lift us from our complacency."
—Ian Hacking

Prickly Paradigm is marketed and distributed by The University of Chicago Press.

www.press.uchicago.edu

A list of current and future titles can be found on our website and at the back of this pamphlet.

www.prickly-paradigm.com

Executive Publisher
Marshall Sahlins

Publishers
Peter Sahlins
Ramona Naddaff
Bernard Sahlins
Seminary Co-op Bookstore

Editor
Matthew Engelke
info@prickly-paradigm.com

David Hahn, Editorial Assistant
Design and layout by Bellwether Manufacturing.

T0083781

The Western Illusion of
Human Nature

The Western Illusion of Human Nature:

With Reflections on the Long History of Hierarchy, Equality, and the Sublimation of Anarchy in the West, and Comparative Notes on Other Conceptions of the Human Condition

Marshall Sahlins

PRICKLY PARADIGM PRESS
CHICAGO

© 2008 Marshall Sahlins
All rights reserved.

Prickly Paradigm Press, LLC
5629 South University Avenue
Chicago, Il 60637

www.prickly-paradigm.com

ISBN: 0-9794057-2-6
ISBN-13: 978-0-9794057-2-3
LCCN: 2008928703

An earlier version of this pamphlet was delivered
as a Tanner Lecture at the University of Michigan
on 4 November 2005.

Printed in the United States of America on acid-free paper.

Notice:

Over the past decade or two, courses on "Western Civilization" have been occupying a progressively smaller place in the curricula of American colleges. Here I attempt to accelerate the trend by reducing "Western Civ" to approximately three hours. My justification is the Nietzschean principle that big issues are like cold baths: one should get into and out of them as quickly as possible.

Time and again for more than two millennia the people we call "Western" have been haunted by the specter of their own inner being: an apparition of human nature so avaricious and contentious that, unless it is somehow governed, it will reduce society to anarchy. The political science of the unruly animal has come for the most part in two contrasting and alternating forms: either hierarchy or equality, monarchial authority or republican equilibrium: either a system of domination that (ideally) restrains people's natural self-interest by an external power; or a self-organizing system of free and equal powers whose opposition (ideally) reconciles their particular interests in the common interest. Beyond politics, this is a totalized metaphysics of order, for the same generic structure of an elemental anarchy resolved by hierarchy or equality is found in the organization of the universe as well as the city, and again in therapeutic concepts of the human body. I claim it is a specifically Western metaphysics, for it supposes an opposition between nature and culture that is distinctive of our own folklore—and contrastive to the many peoples who consider that beasts are basically human rather than humans basically beasts. These peoples could know no primordial "animal nature," let alone one that must be overcome. And they have a point, inasmuch as the modern human species, *Homo sapiens*, emerged relatively recently under the aegis of a much older human culture. By our own paleontological evidence, we too are animal creatures of culture, endowed with the biology of our symbology. The idea that we are involuntary servants of our animal dispositions is an illusion—also originating in the culture.

I am going against the grain of the genetic determinism now so popular in America for its seeming ability to explain all manner of cultural forms by an innate disposition of competitive self-interest. In combination with an analogous Economic Science of autonomous individuals devoted singularly to their own satisfactions by the "rational choice" of everything, not to mention the common native wisdom of the same ilk, such fashionable disciplines as Evolutionary Psychology and Sociobiology are making an all-purpose social science of the 'selfish gene." But as Oscar Wilde said of professors, their ignorance is the result of long study. Oblivious to history and cultural diversity, these enthusiasts of evolutionary egoism fail to recognize the classic bourgeois subject in their portrait of so-called human nature. Or else they celebrate their ethnocentrism by taking certain of our customary practices as proof of their universal theories of human behavior. In this kind of ethnoscience, *l'espèce, c'est moi*—I am the species.

It goes against the current grain too—I mean here the exigent postmodern cravings for indeterminacy—to make extravagant claims for the uniqueness of the Western ideas of man's innate wickedness. I should qualify. Similar notions might well be imagined in state formations elsewhere, insofar as they develop similar interests in controlling their underlying populations. Even Confucian philosophy, for all its suppositions that men are inherently good (Mencius) or inherently capable of the good (Confucius), can come up with alternate views of natural wickedness (Hsün Tzu). Still, I would argue that neither the Chinese nor any other cultural tradition can match the sustained Western contempt for humanity: this long-term scandal of human avarice, together with the antithesis of culture and nature that informs it.

On the other hand, we have not always been so convinced of our depravity. Other concepts of the human being are embedded, for example, in our kinship relations, and they have found certain expressions in our philosophies. Yet we have long been at least half-beast, and that half as a fact of nature has seemed more intractable than any artifice of culture. While I offer no sustained narrative of this lugubrious sense of what we are—no claim of doing an intellectual history, or even an "archaeology"—I put in evidence of its duration the fact that intellectual ancestors from Thucydides through St. Augustine, Machiavelli and the authors of the *Federalist Papers*, right up to our sociobiological contemporaries, have all been accorded the scholarly label of "Hobbesian." Some of these were monarchists, others partisans of democratic republics, yet all shared the same sinister view of human nature.

I begin, however, with the much more robust connection between the political philosophies of Hobbes, Thucydides and John Adams. The curious interrelations of this triad of authors will allow us to sketch the main coordinates of the Metaphysical Triangle of anarchy, hierarchy and equality. For as different as were their solutions to the fundamental problem of human evil, both Hobbes and Adams found in Thucydides' text on the Peloponnesian War, notably his gory account of the revolution at Corcyra, the model of their own ideas of the horrors society would suffer if mankind's natural desires of power and gain were not checked—by a sovereign power said Hobbes, by a balance of power said Adams.

Hobbes and Adams as Thucydideans

In 1763, young John Adams wrote a brief essay titled, "All men would be tyrants if they could." Adams never published the essay, but he revisited it in 1807 to endorse its conclusion that all "simple" (unmixed) forms of government, including pure democracy, as well as all moral virtues, all intellectual abilities, and all powers of wealth, beauty, art and science are no proof against the selfish desires that rage in the hearts of men and issue in cruel and tyrannical government. As he explained the essay's title:

> It means, in my opinion, no more that this plain simple observation upon human nature which every Man, who has ever read a treatise upon Morality, or conversed with the World...must have often made, vis., that the selfish Passions are stronger than the Social, and that the former would always prevail over the latter in any Man, left to the natural Emotions of his own Mind, unrestrained and unchecked by other Power extrinsic to himself.

This sense of the human condition was a life-long conviction of Adams', complemented by the belief that a government of balanced powers was the only way to control the beast. Already in 1767 he claimed that twenty years' investigation of the "secret springs" of human action had more and more persuaded him that "from the Fall of Adam to this time, Mankind in general, has been given up, to strong Delusions, Vile Affections, sordid Lusts and brutal Appetites." These corrupt impulses, moreover, were "stronger than the social." Using a language much like

Thucydides' account of certain incidents of the Peloponnesian War, Adams likewise lamented the vulnerability of civil institutions to the egoistical urges of man's nature. "Religion, superstitions, oaths, education, laws, will all give way before passions, interest and power"—unless and until they are "resisted by passions, interest and power." Hence his long advocacy of a government of counterbalancing powers. By opposing one against another, the destructive dispositions might be turned to beneficial effects. Like many of his educated countrymen, Adams advocated a republican form of Aristotelian or Polybian mixed government, reserving sovereignty to the people while combining democracy, oligarchy and monarchy in a way that realized the virtues and restrained the excesses of each. By counterposing a popularly-elected lower house to a natural aristocracy of wealth in an upper house, the endemic conflict of rich and poor could be neutralized, even as this legislature in general were opposed to and by a single executive authority. Left to itself and human nature, each of these three powers would issue in a self-aggrandizing tyranny; but thus melded together, their self-serving rivalry would preserve the domestic tranquility.

Adams knew the dismal views of Hobbes, Mandeville, Machiavelli and their like on human nature. But for historical evidence, he gave special credence to Thucydides. It seemed to him that when reading Thucydides and Tacitus he was "reading the History of my own times and my own Life." Just so, in the context of the partisan conflicts attending the birth of the American republic, particularly the class conflicts that seemed very similar to those of fifth-century Greece, Thucydides became for Adams the star witness to the havoc that can be caused by out-of-control desires and factional interests. Thus the ancient historian's place front and center in the Preface to Adams' *Defence of the Constitutions of the United States*, where he writes: "It is impossible to read in Thucydides, *lib. iii.* his account of the factions and confusions throughout all Greece, which were introduced by this want of equilibrium, without horror." He then proceeds to give close paraphrase of Thucydides' narrative (3.70-3.85) of the civil strife (*stasis*) at Corcyra.

I radically abbreviate Thucydides' account. It concerns an uprising of "the few" against "the many" in Corcyra: a rebellion of the privileged class against the democratic rule of the people, with the aim of severing the city's allegiance to Athens by establishing an oligarchic regime allied instead with Sparta. In a series of violent clashes, involving also sacrilege against law and religion, each party was victorious in turn, inflicting casualties that mounted progressively when the Spartans intervened on behalf of the oligarchs and the Athenians on the side of the people. In the end, an Athenian fleet established a cordon around the city, whereupon the oligarchic faction suffered bloody massacre at the hands of an out-of-control mob:

> During the seven days that Eurymedon stayed with his sixty [Athenian] ships, the Corcyreans were engaged in butchering those of their fellow-citizens whom they regarded as their enemies, and although the crime imputed was that of attempting to put down the democracy, some were slain also for private hatred, others by their debtors because of the moneys owed to them. Death thus raged in every shape; and, as usually happens at such times, there was no length to which violence did not go; some

were killed by their fathers, and suppliants dragged
from the altar or slain upon it; while some were even
walled up in the temple of Dionysus, and died there.

Apparently more violent than any previous
stasis, the civil war at Corcyra was only the first of the
deadly kind that developed in the context of the
Peloponnesian War. Longstanding conflicts for power
in many cities were exacerbated by the engagement of
the Spartans and Athenians on the side of the oligarchs
and the people respectively. Thucydides' description of
the ensuing breakdown of civil society is similar to his
account of the plague at Athens; indeed he conveys the
sense of an epidemic diffusion of these political
"convulsions," becoming ever more malignant as they
spread from city to city. For the plague here unleashed
was human nature: "human nature, always rebelling
against the law and now its master, gladly showed itself
ungoverned in passion, above respect for justice, and
the enemy of all superiority." "The cause of all these
evils," he said, "was the lust for power arising from
greed and ambition, and from these passions proceded
the violence of the parties engaged in contention." But
when Thucydides asserted that such suffering would
ever be repeated—with varying "symptoms"—"so long
as human nature remained the same," John Adams
broke off his own exposition of the text to say, "if this
nervous historian had known a balance of three powers,
he would not have pronounced the distemper so incur-
able, but would have added—so long as parties in the
cities remained unbalanced."

Yet as Thucydides' description of the "distemper" proceeds, not only did the main institutions of society succumb to human nature, but language itself

suffered a similar degeneration. Moral iniquity was coupled to self-serving hypocrisy to the extent that "words had to change their meaning and take that which was now given to them." In his remarkable work on *Representative Words*, Thomas Gustafson speaks of an archetypal "Thucydidean Moment" when the corruptions of people and language became one. Citing the same passage in Thucydides, Quentin Skinner identified the relevant trope as "paradiastole," referring to morally conflicting valuations of the same term: for example, the way that "democracy" may be perversely defamed by some such term as "mob rule." (For a contemporary example, think of the so-called "compassionate conservatism" of the Bush administration, which gives tax cuts to the rich at the expense of society in the name of "fairness"—they earned it, they deserve it—hence also the definition of the tax on inheritance as a "death tax.") Just so in Corcyra, as words were traduced in the all-out struggle for power, foul became fair, and fair, foul. Cautious plotting masqueraded as "self defense;" prudent hesitation was castigated as "spurious cowardice;" frantic violence was "manliness" and moderation was the lack of it. Oaths were no proof against the advantages of breaking them. The only principle left, observed the classicist W. Robert Conner, was

> the calculation of self-interest. Now all the conventions of Greek life—promises, oaths, supplications, obligations to kin and benefactors and even the ultimate convention, language itself—give way. It is Hobbes' *bellum omnium contra omnes*.

It is indeed—inasmuch as Hobbes was the first to translate Thucydides directly into English from the

Greek. If Thucydides seems Hobbesian, it is because Hobbes was a Thucydidean. In his 1628 translation of *The Peloponnesian War*, Hobbes lauded Thucydides as "the most politic historian that ever writ," putting him in this respect as on a par with Homer in poetry, Aristotle in philosophy, and Demosthenes in oratory. What notably appealed to Hobbes was Thucydides' apparent dislike of democracy and his sustained demonstration of its failures (for so Hobbes chose to read him). Certain of these failures are of special moment here because they stemmed from just those conditions that John Adams thought necessary for the success of a republic, namely, off-setting powers. What Hobbes saw in Thucydides' descriptions of policy-making in Athenian assemblies of the citizens were demagogues serving their own ambitions, "crossing each others' counsels" and thus doing disservice to the city. The debates and debacle of the invasion of Sicily would be a prime example. Hence this bit of doggerel in Hobbes' verse autobiography:

> *Homer* and *Vergil*, *Horace*, *Sophocles*,
> *Plautus*, *Euripides*, *Aristophanes*,
> I understood, nay more; but of all these
> There's none that pleas'd me like *Thucydides*.
> He says Democracy's a Foolish Thing,
> Than a Republick Wiser is one King.

Classical and Hobbesean scholars alike have seen in Thucydides' narrative of the stasis at Corcyra a fundamental source of Hobbes' conception of the state of nature. Writes Terence Bell, for example: "Point for point, feature for feature, Hobbes' state of nature parallels Thucydides' account of the Corcyrean revolution."

Nor do the parallels begin or end there. Even beyond the anarchy of Hobbes' original state—based, as in Thucydides, on man's natural "lust for power arising from greed and ambition" —Hobbes' description of the "incommodities" of the primordial human condition is much like Thucydides' reflections (in the so-called "Archaeology" of Book One) on the origins of the Greeks. Rendered socially disunited and culturally underdeveloped by mutual fears of predation, the first men of Thucydides, like the first men of Hobbes, were without commerce, navigation or cultivation. Destitute of wealth and constantly on the move, the original Greeks built no cities nor "attained to any form of greatness." Likewise for Hobbes, men in the state of nature constructed no "commodious buildings" nor developed any arts, letters or account of time. Instead their lives were famously "solitary, poor, nasty, brutish, and short."

If in John Adams' view the escape from the anarchy described by the "nervous historian" of ancient Greece consisted in a self-regulating system of contending powers, for Thomas Hobbes the solution was a uniquely powerful sovereign who would "keep them all in awe": that is, by coercively restraining and adjudicating the inborn inclination of men to seek their own advantage at the cost of whom it may concern. One might say that the two sages resolved their similarities differently, since Hobbes knew the same reason for government as Adams. Thus Hobbes in *De Cive*:

> I set down for a Principle by experience known to all men, and denied by none, to wit, that the dispositions of men are naturally such, that except they be restrained through fear of some coercive power, every man will distrust and dread every other and as

by natural right he may, so by necessity he will be forced to make use of the strength he has, towards the preservation of himself.

As is often said—and especially well said by C.B. Macpherson in his work on "possessive individual-ism"—Hobbes' narrative of the development from the natural to the political state in *Leviathan* is at the same time an origin myth of capitalist mentality. From the premise of each man's endless desires to secure his own good, there inevitably follows a general scarcity of means, hence mutual incursions in which "the power of one man resisteth and hindereth the effects of the power of another:" again, just what Adams considered a good thing and Hobbes the source of worse to come. Worse was the ensuing evolution of the natural state from a condition of petty bourgeois competition to full-blown capitalist exploitation, as each man finds he can only assure his own good by subduing others and harnessing their powers to his ends. Parenthetically it might be noted here that although Hobbes was a great critic of the abuse of words, his observation that all kinds of ostensible acts, including praiseworthy ones, are really so many ways of gaining power over others, amounts to the functional equivalent of paradiastole. Liberality, affa-bility, nobility or "what quality soever make a man beloved, or feared of many, or the reputation of such quality, is power, because it is a means to have the assis-tance, and service of many." One is reminded of the current obsession with "power" among social scientists and cult studs, a kind of *power functionalism* that likewise dissolves the most diverse cultural forms in an acid bath of domination-effects. (This also demonstrates Hobbes' point that one of the things that should be amended in universities is "the frequency of insignificant speech.") But to return to the original Hobbesean state: guided by reason and driven by fear, men finally agree to surrender their private right to use force in favor of a sovereign power who will bear their person and exercise their strength in the interest of collective peace and defense. Although this sovereign power could be an assembly, after the experience of parliamentary hubris and the regicide of Charles the First, it seemed clear to Hobbes that, divine right apart, "wiser is one king."

Contraries, said Aristotle, are the sources of their contraries. This opposition of hierarchy to equality, monarchy to republic, is itself dialectical: the one being defined against the other historically, in practical politics as well as ideological debate. There is always the motivation of the immediate context: Adams' was participating in a rebellion against the British crown; Hobbes' absolutism was conditioned by the attacks on royalty's prerogatives. But beyond that, our authors take their respective places in a centuries-long Western dispute between popular and monarchial sovereignty, engaging the arguments of distant philosophical adversaries and by-gone political constitutions. Adams took Hobbes himself for a respected interlocutor: "Hobbes, a man, however unhappy in his temper, or detestable for his principles, equal in genius and learning to any of his contemporaries." Whereas for his part, Hobbes' royalism, as Quentin Skinner shows, responded intertextually to republican doctrines of ancient memory: to Roman and Renaissance theories of civic order, with their emphasis on the citizens' equal voice in government. One of Hobbes' aspirations in *Leviathan*, writes Skinner, "is to demolish this entire structure of [republican] thought, and with it the theory of equality and citizen-

ship on which humanist civil science had been raised."
Moreover, it only stands to (Hegelian) reason that each
of the contraries preserves and encompasses the other in
its negation, equality in hierarchy and vice versa. The
way that Hobbes initiates the state of nature with each
man's equal right to everything—which, as leading to
continual war, is the trouble with it; even as Adams fore-
sees an end to the war of nature in tyranny—which is
the trouble with it. This "entire structure of thought"
should include Hobbes' absolutism as the historic
complement of the republicanism he wanted to demolish. It is a diachronic and dynamic structure of interde-
pendent contraries: two contrasting modes of cultural
order, alternating with each other over a long time.

Then again, as regimes for restraining the
unruly human animal, sovereign domination and
republican balance stand together in the cultural side of
the fundamental nature-culture dualism that grounds
this "entire structure." Nature is the necessity: the pre-
social, anti-social egoism with which culture must cope.
Or to which it must succumb, the way that at Corcyra
cultural order dissolved in the maelstrom unleashed by
out-of-control desires of power and gain. This culture-
nature antithesis is as old and continuous as the notions
of governance it underwrites: older than Thucydides,
we shall see, and as current as the selfish gene.

Clearly, in speaking mainly of these three,
Thucydides, Hobbes and Adams, I merely allegorize.
The same politics of human self-contempt have been
advocated by many famous and not-so-famous people.
"Man is an animal that requires a master," said Kant,
admitting however that the case was hopeless inasmuch
as "the master is himself an animal, and needs a master."
Or again, to take a seemingly bizarre leap: appalled by

the racial and draft riots of 1863 in New York City, Herman Melville reproduces in verse the lineaments of the stasis at Corcyra:

> The town is taken by its rats—ship rats
> And rats of the wharves. All civil charms
> And priestly spells which late held hearts in Awe—
> Fear-bound, subjected to a better sway
> Than sway of self; these like a dream dissolve,
> And man rebounds whole aeons back to nature...

Melville speaks not only to natural anarchy, but to its remedy by sovereign authority. Behind the strong-arm put down of the riots by Union forces, Melville perceived a dictatorial Abraham Lincoln, who in the guise of a "wise Draco" practiced the "cynic tyrannies of honest kings," violating republican harmony and any faith in human goodness.

Still, as it thus engages human nature, our allegory extends far beyond the political. Indeed the same dynamic scheme can be found in diverse cultural registers from the elementary composition of matter to the structure of the cosmos, passing by way of therapeutic concepts of the body and harmonious arrangements of the city. We have to do with a veritable metaphysics of order than can be traced back to deep antiquity and abstractly described as the transformation of the oppugnancy of self-aggrandizing individual elements into a stable collective, either by the constraining action of an external power holding the fractious elements in place, or by the elements themselves holding each other in check. Here is a structure of *longue durée*: a recurrent and dynamic metaphysics of anarchy, hierarchy and equality.

Ancient Greece

It is as if Thucydides had lifted his description of the anarchy at Corcyra from Hesiod's lament for the state of humanity in his own degenerate "Age of Iron," when justice was likewise in abeyance and a natural inclination of ruthless competition was unleashed. Some four centuries before Thucydides, Hesiod's *Works and Days* spoke of the same violations of kinship and morality, the same "crooked words" and "lying oaths," the same lust of power and gain, the same violence and destruction. In the Age of Iron:

> Father will have no common bond with son,
> Neither will guest with host, nor friend with friend;
> The brother-love of past days will be gone.
> Men will dishonour parents....
> Wretched and godless, they
> Refusing to repay their bringing up,
> Will cheat their aged parents of their due.
> Men will destroy the towns of other men.
> The just, the good, the man who keeps his word
> Will be despised, but men will praise the bad
> And insolent. Might will be Right, and shame
> Will cease to be. Men will do injury
> To better men by speaking crooked words
> And adding lying oaths; and everywhere
> Harsh-voiced and sullen-faced and loving harm,
> Envy will walk along with wretched men.

Comments classicist Gerald Naddaf: "Without justice, Hesiod believed that people will devour themselves like animals; there will be a sort of Hobbesian state of nature—not unlike what preceded the reign of Zeus."

Hobbes is getting older and older. He is also getting less and less original, considering that Naddaf's reference is to the creation of universal peace and order by the sovereign god Zeus upon subduing the rebellious Titans—who are represented in tradition as the archetype of human nature. As Detienne and Vernant put it in their dazzling commentary on Hesiod's *Theogony*, where this structure is famously narrated: "There is no cosmic order without differentiation, hierarchy and supremacy, but there is no supremacy without conflict, injustice and violence." Beginning in criminality and rebellion among the gods, thus a formlessness of society that corresponds to an initial amorphous state of the universe, the story ends in a stable cosmos under the sovereignty imposed by the victorious Zeus, with its differentiated realms of heaven, earth and underworld. Only that, the resolution of disorder having been wrought by force rather than by contract, the narrative is in this respect more Nietzschean than Hobbesian. In Nietzsche's vision of the origin of the commonwealth, violent conquest and ruthless despotism were required to impose order on the original brutish population:

> I have used the word "commonwealth," but it should be clearly understood what I mean: a pack of savages, a race of conquerors, themselves organized for war and able to organize others, fiercely dominating a population perhaps vastly superior in numbers, yet amorphous and nomadic. Such was the beginning of the human polity.

Just so, in the *Theogony*, order was won in a relentless battle of ten years that set the younger generation of the gods led by Zeus against his father Cronus and the unruly Titans, with the governance of the universe at stake. Aided by his cunning intelligence and overwhelming power, Zeus finally gained the victory, casting the Titans in chains to misty Tartarus below. After a second triumph over a dangerous rebel (Typhon), Zeus apportioned the honors and privileges of the gods, their statuses and functions. Under the sovereignty of Zeus, this divine government was now and forever stable; for thenceforth quarrels among the immortals would be settled by binding oaths. If by contrast humans notoriously break their oaths, as at Corcyra, it is because strife, misery and evil were banished to the earthly plane. Such is the human lot, tempered only by Zeus' gift of justice and the feckless hope he sent to mankind along with the "beautiful evil," Pandora, in the same jar that brought the miseries.

Of particular interest here are the traditional relations of common nature between the Titanic and human races, because they thus ground the Western sense of the political as a constraint on the antisocial individual in a folklore of ancient standing. "The Titan," Paul Ricoeur observed, "is the figure through which human evil is rooted in prehuman evil." In Orphic myth, humans indeed descend from the ashes of Titans buried by Zeus for murdering Dionysus. Their disorderly titanic dispositions show up in Plato's *Laws*, in the passage where he warns that unruly music will encourage unwanted democratic license, until "the spectacle of the Titanic nature of which our old legends speak is reenacted; man returns to the old condition of a hell of unending misery." (Should we blame Elvis and the Beatles for our present problems?)

If men were Titans by nature, their ancient kings were manifestations of Zeus by ancestry. Cosmogony endures in the form of dynasty. Old foundational legends of Peloponnesian states tell of immigrant heroes, born of a union of Zeus with a mortal woman, who marry the daughters of autochthonous rulers and usurp the kingship. The origin of the state is a terrestrial version of the generation of the universe from the cosmic union of Heaven (Uranus) and Earth (Gaia). The eponymous Lacedaemon, Zeus-born stranger, marries the eponymous Sparta, offspring of earth-born rulers, thus establishing a civilizing dynasty among the inhabitants of the Eurotas plain—and their eternal identity. Agamemnon, King of Mycenae, was likewise a royal descendant of Zeus, whence came his authority over the other kings of his great army. But by Homer's time, anything like a faithful human copy of the universal sovereignty of Zeus had already disappeared from Greece four or five hundred years before, with the destruction of the ancient Mycenaean kingdoms. True that traces of royalty marked by divinity remained in the epics of the eighth-century poets. The justice of certain good rulers in Hesiod's Works and Days could not only prosper the city but engender the prosperity of nature. Still, the kings of Hesiod's era were not only much reduced in power compared to their long-gone (but not forgotten) Mycenaean predecessors, their authority was being contested and divided by rivalrous elites. In *Archaeology as Cultural History*, his excellent summary of the prehistory of the classical city-state, Ian Morris provides an account of this aristocratic competition, noting its coincidence with the reopening of elite trade with the Orient after the so-called "Dark Age" that followed the Mycenaean

collapse. Verily, the agonistic spirit was not only pervasive among the warring nobility but largely abroad in
the society, according to J.-P. Vernant. Quoting Hesiod,

> Potter hates potter, carpenters compete,
> And beggar strives with beggar, bard with bard,

Vernant draws the interesting inference that the competition presupposes a certain equality among the adversaries, even as it aims at hierarchy. Or as one might say,
the emergent antithesis, hierarchy, encompasses its
suppressed negation, equality. It seems that something
like that was surfacing in the aristocratic contentions
with royal or tyrannical rule. Well before it was
achieved in the Athenian democracy of the fifth-
century, the demand for political equality, *isonomia*, was
raised by the nobility of certain archaic city-states—
who were losing out in their chronic competition for
supremacy. *Isonomia*, "equality," was the reclamation of
certain oligarchs protesting their disenfranchisement by
tyrants. (Something like the Magna Carta, perhaps.)
Kurt Raatlaub even speaks of *isonomia* as an "aristocratic concept," one of the "aristocratic values."

Eventually the opposition of equality to hierarchy settles out politically as the conflict between popular sovereignty on one side and oligarchy or monarchy
on the other: in which form, along with many cultural
entailments, it will run through Western history for
better than two thousand years. Morris thus speaks of a
certain "middling ideology" that emerged in the eighth
century and struggled fitfully with a system of aristocratic power until its triumph in the institution of
Athenian democracy. The social history of the archaic
period, he writes, "is best understood as a conflict

between these antithetical cultures." The "middlers" were partisans of a self-organizing, egalitarian and participatory regime. In invidious contrast to the heroic aristocracy, they represented a philosophy of living within the mean. They would keep bodily appetites under control, eschew greed and hubris, and in that way maintain solidarity with their fellows. As Morris puts it, they comprised an "imagined community" of moderate, equal male citizens, turned away from the past and the east. Whereas the aristocrats, taking the old Mycenaean nobility for their model, looked above and beyond the society of their compatriots for their identity as well as their authority. Their status came from the gods, from heroic ancestors and from the Orient—whence they imported the material intimations of their divinity.

Given the differences of these "antithetical cultures," their cohabitation in the developing city-states could convert them into antagonistic factions, joining the elite against the populace in struggles that were increasingly perceived as conflicts of rich and poor. Plutarch relates that Solon's friend Ancharsis laughed at him "for thinking he could check the injustice and rapacity of the citizens by written laws," laws that had no more strength than spiders' webs and would be torn to pieces by the rich and powerful. At issue were the measures proposed by the famous Athenian law-giver early in the sixth century, allowing the poor relief from debts and punishments and broadening participation in a government that was favoring the privileged. Solon replied to his friend that men will keep their agreements when neither party sees it will profit by breaking them, and that he was working to make it more advantageous to all concerned to practice justice. Perhaps like later statesmen Solon hoped to make it more advantageous to acknowledge the rights of political adversaries than to raise sedition and plunge the city into disorder. In any event, in speaking to the rapacity of the citizens, the vulnerability of law to self-interest, the opposition of hierarchy and equality and the remedy of balancing the powers, the argument, supposing something like it took place, suggests that the Western metaphysics of order was present at the formation of the classical *polis*.

The fifth century saw further versions of the old opposition of hierarchy and equality, culminating in their ideological inflation in the course of the Peloponnesian War. Although, following Ian Morris, we can date the triumph of democratic ideals to the Athenian constitution of 507 BC, civil wars between the elite and populist factions continued to trouble many Greek cities for more than a century. Originally aristocratic, the elite during this time were more and more defined as plutocrats. Plato says in *The Republic* that any city is many cities, for in the first place it is divided into a *polis* of the rich and a *polis* of the poor, which are constantly at war, and these are again divided into smaller contending groups. During the Peloponnesian War, as we have seen, this endemic strife was subsumed in a general, pan-Hellenic confrontation of the "democracy" supported by the Athenians and the "oligarchy" of the Spartans—reconstituted forms, as it were, of the archaic "antithetical cultures." Initially attested by Herodotus in the mid-fifth-century, the terms "democracy" and "oligarchy" first appear as ideological causes-to-die-for precisely in Thucydides' description of the Athenian and Spartan interventions in the stasis at Corcyra. But by then the beneficent slogan of Athenian imperialism, *isonomia*, "equality," had invaded cosmologies as well as polities; and it was working its way into corpologies and ontologies, systems of the body and fundamental concepts of the nature of things.

Isonomia, "the fairest of names," Herodotus called it. In principle, the *isonomia* of which Athens was the model entailed equal participation of the (male) citizens in a government they held in common and ruled as a sovereign body met in the Assembly. Since women, slaves and resident foreigners were excluded from these privileges, the democracy was in fact supported by extra-constitutional forms of hierarchy, some quite authoritarian. (Even apart from a history of slavery, the same contradictions remain true for contemporary Americans who are pleased to believe they "live in a democracy" although they spend the far greater part of their lives in undemocratic institutions such as families, schools, capitalist workplaces—not to mention the military and bureaucratic organizations of government itself. Hey look, people: the democracy has no clothes.) For the Athenian citizens, *isonomia* meant equality before the law, equality of voice and vote in the Assembly and equal opportunity to participate in the Council of Five Hundred (the *Boule*) that set the agenda for the Assembly and exercised important diplomatic and judicial functions. In the Council, each of the ten tribes established by Cleisthenes' constitution of 507 was represented by 50 men who were selected by lot for a term of one year. Each tribal delegation served in rotation as the presiding and standing committee of the whole for a period of 36 or 37 days. This rotational equality is an interesting form for its subsumption of hierarchy in and as the principle of *isonomia*. (We shall see the like in Hippocratic medicine.) The rotation fulfills the happy Aristotelian ideal of a government in which the citizens rule and are ruled by turns.

Taking the Mycenean and Minoan kingdoms of yore as a basis of comparison, the transformation in the character of sovereignty from monarchy to democracy was multiple and radical. To adopt Vernant's description of the contrast: ruled privately, coercively and mystically from the palace above, the ancient kingdoms eventually gave way to a *polis* in which the powers of government devolved collectively, equally and publicly on the citizens. Assembled openly in the center of the city (the *agora*), the citizens determine by reason and persuasion the policies that reconcile their private interests with each other in the interest of what is good for the state—again, in principle. Writes Vernant:

> The human group now sees itself in the following way: alongside the private, individual houses there is a center where public matters are debated, and this center represents all that is "common," the collectivity as such. Human society no longer forms, as it did within mythical space, a world on different levels with the king on top and beneath him a whole social hierarchy where status is defined in terms of domination and submission. Now the universe of the city-state is one of egalitarian and reversible relationships in which all the citizens are defined in relation to one another as being equal.

Still, for all the reciprocity, equality, and collectivity, the democratic polis remained vulnerable to the disruptive effects of its citizens' self-concerns. Of this the Athenians were too well aware. Speaking of "the self-advantage which every creature by its nature perceives as a good, while by convention of law it is forcibly diverted to paying honor to equality," the sophist Glaucon in *The Republic* evokes the same opposition between law (or culture) and self-interest (or nature) that marked Thucydides' description of the civil war at Corcyra. Such opposition between private and public good was, in the view of P.J. Brunt, "the origin of the internal conflicts… so prevalent in Greek cities, and therefore of the development of Greek political theory." For another example, Pericles' injunction in the "Funeral Oration" regarding the necessary civic virtue of the citizens: they should know that their private welfare is best served by promoting the interests of the city—an appropriate sentiment when memorializing men died in battle. Pericles' well-meant maxim was destined to be rehearsed by leading statesmen in republics ever after, which at least proves it was as often needed. But then, in the sixth century BC, well before Plato and Pericles worried the political problem, Anaximander of Miletus had made the governing of self-interest by the interaction of equal and opposed forces the principle of good order in the whole universe.

Rather than a cosmos ordered from above by an all-powerful god, Anaximander's universe was a self-regulating natural system, internally controlled by the compensating give-and take of the equal elements of which it was composed. Be it noted that the surviving body of Anaximander's work is fragmentary, and its obscurities have been the subject of much exegesis: including, in the modern era, some not very enlightening comment by Nietzsche and a Heideggerean riff in the presencing of being. Still, the contrast to the cosmos organized and dominated by Zeus is clear enough and remarked by many—notably by Charles H. Kahn in his thorough study of the Anaximander corpus in the context of the pre-Socratic philosophies.

"Anaximander," Kahn writes, "denies that any elemental body or portion of the world dominates another; for him it is equality and equilibrium which characterize the world."

Right from the cosmogonic beginning, Anaximander ruled out the possibility that any one ontological element generates or dominates the others. The universe arises neither from water nor any other of the so-called elementary substances, but from "some different, boundless nature [*apeiron*]" that produces the heavens and the worlds within them. By the usual scholarly interpretation, the elementary components differentiated out of the infinite (*apeiron*) are binary opposites such as hot and cold, moist and dry; these are in contentious opposition to one another, although being equal, no one is able to overcome the others. Instead the elements make reparations for their unjust invasions of each other, a process that generates existing things—albeit that in the course of time all such things resolve again into their elementary constituents. In a seminal article on "*Isonomia*," Gregory Vlastos observed that Anaximander's solution to the problem of cosmic justice, modeled on civic-political justice, was thereby completely different from aristocratic or monarchial justice in Hesiod. Rather, Anaximander's universal order "answers substantially to *Isonomia*, for it assumes that the only reliable preservative of justice in a community is the equal distribution of power among its members."

A similar sense of the constitution of order out of the contestation of equal elements obtains in Anaximander's larger cosmography, where the earth is fixed at the center of the universe by its equidistance from the fiery bodies of the celestial sphere. Here again eternal stability is achieved without benefit of external sovereignty. The equipoise seems not only a function of equal distances but of conflicting forces, particularly as concerns the earth, inasmuch the universe is cold and moist at its earthly center and hot and dry in its heavenly periphery. Further, as classicists have frequently noted, this cosmic politics of the fixed earth resembles the spatial order of the democratic *polis*, with its many households surrounding the central *agora*, where their several interests are reciprocally met and mutually adjusted.

In the microcosm as it is in the macrocosm: within the healthy bodies of denizens of these households, *isonomia* also reigned. For health, according to the foundational treatise of the late-sixth century physician Alcmaeon of Croton, consists precisely in the "*isonomia*" or "equal rights" of the contending powers making up the body. (The texts on Alcmaeon list hot and cold, bitter and sweet, moist and dry among these bodily powers, but there were probably more.) On the other hand, "monarchy" or the domination of any one power over the others was the cause of disease and destruction in Alcmaeon's treatise. Among the numerous testaments to the long-running currency of this *isonomic* corpology is the disquisition in Plato's *Timaeus* on disease as caused by an "unnatural" excess, deficit or change of place among the four natures of which the body is constructed—that is, earth, fire, water and air. In an analogous context, Charles Kahn remarked there is practically no limit to the number of texts that could be cited in illustration of the view of nature as "a dynamic interplay between conflicting forces," and he singles out the Hippocratic successors of Alcmaeon as most exemplary of this "fifth-century naturalism."

The humoral medicine of the Hippocratic physicians greatly expanded and complicated the functioning of balance by bringing environmental, temporal, temperamental and other factors into play, while at the same time the doctors' allopathic treatments made such balance a principle of practice as well as of theory. In the early Hippocratic treatise on *The Nature of Man*, the humors (for example, *phlegm*) are linked to the seasons (in this case winter) by the mediation of a common primary element (cold). Health would consist, then, in a system of rotational equality with each of the four humors—phlegm, blood, yellow and black bile—prevailing it its appropriate season. Hippocratic treatments, moreover, consisted of prescribing the contrary of the element out of proportion, such as food deemed cold for the cure of fevers or warm baths for dry coughs. A crucial implication of this principle of allopathy—which incidentally is still in therapeutic use—is that medicine joins politics as an arena in which *isonomia* is a *praxis*: that is, a pragmatic and desirable principle of action. This helps explain how the humoral medicine of the Hippocratic doctors, as further elaborated by the second-century AD physician Galen, could be reproduced complete with political allusion as late as the eighteenth century by that famous apostle of the balance of powers, John Adams. "Some physicians," he wrote, "have thought if it were possible to keep the several humors of the body in exact balance, it might be immortal; and so perhaps would a political body, if the balance of power could always be exactly even." This is what you call a "structure of the long run."

Another is Empedocles' famous doctrine of the four "roots": fire, air, water and earth, the elements that make up all existing things. The sixth-century philosophers and physicians were already developing theories of the formation of things out of opposed primordial elements such as hot and cold, heavy and light, moist and dry. Empedocles (495-435) meant to limit the elements to four, which interestingly enough he first characterized in a hierarchical register as gods; although it was from their nature as equal substances, brought together and separated by the equal and contrarian forces of Love and Strife, that everything was compounded, from trees and persons to birds, beasts and the immortal gods themselves. Here was a general metaphysics of what there is: an ontology that like the Anaximandrian universe, the Hippocratic body or the Athenian democracy is based on the give-and-take of equal qualities or forces. Or as Heraclitus' maxim has it: "Opposition brings concord. Out of discord comes the fairest harmony."

As a principle of order, *isonomia* was dominant in fifth-century Athens, but of course it did not exclude hierarchical thinking, then or after, particularly among the philosophical masters. (Indeed the ancient Greek dualisms seem to defy Levi-Strauss's observation that binary opposites are characteristically ranked and likely unstable. Then again, the ideal of the absolute equality of opposed elements may be the problem with them, so far as practice is concerned, and not only in ancient Greece.) Plato's *Statesman* and *Timaeus* offer theories of world order structurally like that imposed by the sovereign Zeus upon defeating the disorderly Titans. All things composed in whole or in part of matter, or all visible things, have a natural tendency to fall into "discordant and disorderly motion," thus their original state is one of anarchy, until they are taken in hand by

God. "God implanted in them proportions both sever-
ally in relations to themselves and in their relations to
one another, so far as it was in any way possible for
them to be in harmony." Or again, Aristotle's famous
cosmology, while likewise rendered abstract by the
purge of ancient mythical figures, similarly renders
them homage by retaining the sense of a divinely established world order with a supreme source in the
Unmoved Mover. The Unmoved Mover imparts the
eternal motion of the highest celestial sphere, which in
turn gives impetus to a pantheon of lesser movers of
lower spheres, down to the mover that moves the
changeable sublunar things.

In the same vein but in a human-political register, living in an Athens long committed to *isonomia* did
not prevent Plato from imagining a Republic governed
by an elite of the well-educated and well-born. Their
own wisdom, virtue and self-control would enable the
ruling Guardians to hold down the meaner desires of
the many. By virtue of their own self-mastery they
could master the motley catalogue of appetites, pleasures and pains that Plato attributed to women, children, slaves and "the base rabble of those who are free
men in name." For in the tripartite soul of the well-
educated, the rational part, aided by the spiritual part,
is able to rule over the concupiscent soul, which in
everyone is the largest part and "by nature most insatiable of gain." Spirit and reason must keep guard over
appetite and lust. Or else, waxing great with bodily
pleasures, "the concupiscent soul, no longer confined
to her own sphere, shall attempt to enslave and rule
those not her natural-born subjects and overturn the
whole life of man." Note here the subsumed politics of
balance required for the health of the hierarchical soul.

Note too that the concupiscent soul takes *her* place between Pandora and Eve in an old matrilineal genealogy of blame for the baleful cupidity of men. And note finally that the opposition between the trained-up rational soul and the naturally insatiable concupiscent soul reproduces in the microcosm the same antithesis of convention and natural self interest that we have seen in Thucydides and others. And we have yet to see that despite his antipathy to the sophists of his day, Plato's soul science in this regard follows their usual distinctions of nature and culture—as also did Aristotle's.

Whether in the dominant mode of an egalitarian metaphysics or in the subdominant system of hierarchy, the same notion of the resolution of an underlying conflict of elements is at large throughout ancient Greek culture. However, when it comes to determining which is the prime mover among the relevant cultural domains, the classicists, working on vaguely Durkheimian or Marxian principles of theory arising out of social practice, nearly all agree that politics is the fundamental condition. The cosmological, the physiological, etc., are reflexes of the political. In particular it is claimed that with the emergence of the democratic city, *isonomia* then prevailed over *monarchia* in the ideas of nature as it had actually triumphed in the practices of society. Nature was modeled on the egalitarian city-state, the way Anaximander's cosmos, for example, appears to mirror the earthly *polis*. Among other problems, however, this simplifying reduction allows no account of the complex temporalities and dialectics that were historically in play.

Isonomia, as we know, was very possibly an aristocratic value in the first place, and in any case as an ideal it was as much a precondition of the democratic *polis* of the late sixth century as it was a consequence thereof. (The principle here is Marx's own to the effect that the worst of architects is better than the best of bees, because the former is able to erect the building in his imagination before he erects it in reality.) Nor could there be any simple correlation between *isonomia* in the city and balanced opposition in nature. Alcmaeon's system of the body may have been democratic, based on the "equal rights" of its components, but his homeland was not: Croton was then a narrow oligarchy, notable for serious inequities. Clearly, *isonomia* was not just a "superstructure" to a practical "infrastructure." Like certain famous turtles "all the way down," it was in all the structures, down to the fundamental nature of things. It was in the cultural basis.

The critical point is that for the ancient Greeks the boundaries between society and nature were not as rigidly demarcated or analytically policed as they are in the modern scholarly imagination. Alcmaeon describes an unbalanced, diseased condition of the body in political terms; Thucydides describes a disharmonious condition of the city in terms of disease. Sir Ernest Barker provides a Pythagorean example of a natural basis of the political, derived from the proposition that justice is a square number. A square number is perfect harmony, since it is composed of equal parts, and the number of parts is equal to the numerical value of each part. "It follows that justice is based on the conception of a state composed of equal parts." In Euripides' *Phoenician Women* a similar argument appears in Jocasta's plea to her son Etocles that he share the rule of the state with his brother Polyneices:

Equality set up men's weights and measures.
gave them their numbers. And night's sightless eye
equal divides with day the circling year...
So sun and night are servants to mankind
Yet you will not endure to hold your house
In even shares with him? Where's justice then?

Charles Kahn points out that such interchangeability of society and nature was traditional in Greek antiquity. What certain fifth-century philosophers were moved to establish, he says, was their separation. More specifically, society and nature were defined as contraries "as a result of certain fifth-century controversies regarding *physis* [nature] and *nomos* [convention]." Here was the dualism that established the natural ground of our Metaphysical Triangle: the pre-social, anti-social human nature that the cultural systems of equality and hierarchy themselves contend to control.

The sophists were the usual suspects. Speaking of the "tenacious lineage" of the *nomos-physis* dualism in the political culture of the West, Giorgio Agamben observes:

The Sophistic polemic against nomos in favor of nature (which developed with ever increasing urgency during the course of the Fourth Century) can be considered the necessary premise of the opposition between the state of nature and the "commonwealth" which Hobbes posits as the ground of his conception of sovereignty.

Of course the lineage should also include Thucydides who was an inspiration to Hobbes and an auditor of the sophists, particularly Gorgias and Antiphon. Not to forget the more remote ancestors, for the sophists were hardly the first to draw fateful inferences from the conflict of human nature and the city, although their predecessors need not have employed the *physis-nomos* categories as such or in their fifth-century acceptation. A vicious and avaricious humanity had been the enemy of good order at least since Hesiod. Then there were the poets. "Nature willed it, who cares naught for law," read a Euripidian fragment. Conversely, in Sophocles' *Antigone*, the law of the city cares naught for the sentiments of the family. Here is a question of kinship we will need to revisit, as also the general contrarian principle of a good nature, bad culture therein implied. Of all the possible permutations of the *nomos-physis* dualism, depending on which of the two is privileged as the good thing and which is thought to impose itself on the other, the "Rousseauean" sense of a pure nature and a corrupt culture has run second only to its "Hobbesian" contrary in the longer course of Western history—or indeed, it has been carried along with the latter, in the way the original Edenic condition of man is evoked by the notorious fall into evil. Still, since the late fifth-century BC, as Agamben indicates, our native anthropology has hewed tenaciously and returned consistently to the sophists' darker views of human nature. Devoted singularly to his own good and driven to brutal competition with his fellows, this is the beast with whom culture must cope—too often unsuccessfully.

What chance did culture have if it were just local, changeable matters of belief and custom, in comparison to behavioral dispositions that were hardwired in the species and imperatives of each individual? "Things fair and things just," as Aristotle put it, "are characterized by so much diversity that they come to seem fine by custom [*nomos*] and not by nature [*physis*]." Aristotle was no sophist, of course, but he was a big fan of the natural, of its authenticity or even its legitimacy; hence his perception, shared by many, of cultural difference as the evidence of a merely human agency by contrast to the self-determination of natural things. The properties of natural things are beyond fashioning by human intention or habituation. Throw a stone in the air a thousand times, it will not stay aloft but necessarily descend to earth in conformity with its essential nature. Arthur Lovejoy and George Boas observe that by Aristotle's time, *physis* had come to signify "in the vocabulary of cosmology and meta-physics the objective qualities or independent realities of the external world, and hence to express the abstract concept of objectivity." Indeed two thousand years before the idea of invariant "laws of nature" was devel-oped in the scientific culture of the West, it had already been coined as such in antiquity—specifically in refer-ence to the desires of stronger persons or parties to dominate and take advantage of weaker. Such was "nature's own law" argued the sophist Callicles in the *Gorgias*, and Thucydides has the Athenians saying something very similar to the hapless Melians they were besieging—texts that will come up again presently. Note that as an independent realm of neces-sity, *physis* is thus subjectless—except possibly as god created the world—and accordingly in humans it refers to aspects of behavior for which they are not responsi-ble: the inherent and involuntary urgings of man's makeup. The absence of subjects is a distinctive quality of the Western imagination of "nature," again in contrast to the many other peoples who live in worlds imbued with subjectivity, their cosmos being populated with the sun, moon, stars, animals, mountains, thunder, food crops and other such non-human persons.

In the ancient Greek view, *nomos*, as the stuff of human action, is known and practiced subjectively. Hence its contingency and instability—and even its inferiority to nature on the score of reality. Speaking of a sophistic argument he is setting up for dismantling, the Athenian in the *Laws* says of the late-born human creation, art, as compared to nature:

> Art...herself as perishable as her creations, has since given birth to certain toys with little real substance to them, simulacra as shadowy as the arts themselves, such as those which spring from painting, music, and other fellow crafts....Statesmanship in especial, they say, is a thing which has little in common with nature, but is mainly a business of art; legislation likewise is altogether an affair not of nature but of art, and its positions are unreal.

Whether art, law, politics or custom in general, such man-made *nomoi* have all the attributes of (Lockean) secondary qualities of perception, like hot and cold, bitter and sweet. But what proved worst of all for the subsequent career of the culture concept in native Western thought was that *nomos* acquired the sense of something false in comparison to the authenticity and reality of nature. Man-made and artificial, culture was not true in the way nature was. Lovejoy and Boas write:

> It was obviously an ethically significant phenomenon in linguistic history when the expression [*nomos*] that usually meant either "by law" or "in accordance with

accepted mores" also took on the sense, not only of "subjectivity," but of the latter adverb with an unfavorable connotation, i.e., erroneously.

That nature is true and culture is false motivates the complementary long-term anthropologies that I oversimply spoke of as Rousseauean and Hobbesian, both privileging nature over culture while taking antithetical senses of the natural. The one view, that nature is pure and good but generally in thrall to culture, has persisted in nostalgic visions of the golden age of Cronus, the Garden of Eden and the Noble Savage— the last occasionally reported to be still extant in America and Tahiti in early modern times. Hippocratic and Galenic medicine also lent their practice to this idea, inasmuch as they conceived health to be the natural state of the body and treatment to consist of correcting an unnatural balance or letting nature take its course. The authenticity of human nature lay behind appeals to natural law and to a range of meliorative and sometimes utopian positions on natural human rights and universal morality. Lately the beneficence of nature, again by negation to the corruption of culture, has resurfaced as a commodity value in the form of organic food products and bottled water from pure springs in "primitive" Fiji—which in its plastic containers perhaps does make a good culture, for bacteria. The complementary, dismal view of human nature has had the greater structural entailments, as can be seen in the variety of relations between natural avarice and cultural order conceived by the sophists and their fellow traveler in this regard, Thucydides. They virtually set the theoretical agenda for mainstream Western social thought for all the centuries since.

Unlike Protagoras' faith that with the god's help men's sense of justice and mutual respect would curb their anti-social inclinations, most of these arguments were fairly cynical. For an extreme example: Thrasymachus' might-is-right irruption in *The Republic*, where he claims that "the just is nothing else than the advantage of the stronger." By this argument, society itself, in its own structure, is the direct reflection of the self-interest of the strongest party, whether this be the many as in democracies, the few in oligarchies, or the one in tyrannies. Thus again, the orator Lysias: "The first thing to keep in mind is that no man is by nature an oligarch or a democrat, but each strives to set up the kind of constitution that would be to his advantage." The implication is rather like the Benthamite principle that society is nothing more than the arrangements sedimented out of men's pursuit of their own best interests. More complex and up-to-date sociobiologically speaking, not least for its appeal to animal precedents, is Callicas' complex spiel in the *Gorgias* to the effect that institutions of good order and noble sentiment are merely mystifications of natural self-love, and all the more fragile for it. These ostensibly good *nomoi* are weapons of the many weak in an all round struggle for advantage with the stronger few. By promoting justice and fair play, thus passing off their private interest as collective right-thinking, the weaker majority secures an advantage it does not naturally deserve, insofar as it has been able to shame and impede the few from exercising their greater strength. Still, says Callicas, where what is right by nature becomes in this way wrong by convention, society will be vulnerable to the greater law of domination by him who can. Whether we speak of animals, states or races of mankind, nature makes it plain that it is right for the stronger to have the advantage over the weaker, the better over the worse, the more able over the less:

> For what justification had Xerxes in invading Greece or his father in invading Scythia? And there are countless similar instances one might mention. But I imagine that these men act in accordance with the true nature of right, yes and, by heaven, according to nature's own law, though not perhaps by the law we frame. We mold the best and strongest among ourselves, catching them like young lion cubs, and by spells and incantations we make slaves of them, saying that they must be content with equality, and that this is what is right and fair. But if a man arises endowed with a nature sufficiently strong, he will, I believe shake off all these controls, burst his fetters, and break loose. And trampling upon our scraps of paper, our spells and incantations, and all our unnatural conventions, he rises up and reveals himself our master who was our slave and then shines forth nature's true justice.

When in Thucydides' famous "Melian Dialogue" the Athenians invoke the same law of domination, one would think that "human nature" had already achieved its modern Western function as a portmanteau excuse for ethically problematic cultural practices—such as the subordination of women, serial monogamy or the love of money. By blaming the negative aspect on nature, the moral contradiction—as between imperialism and democratic equality (*isonomia*)—is placed beyond anyone's responsibility, most particularly those who are indulged by it. Just so, the

Athenians spoke as if they had no choice but to rule the weaker Melians. For their imperial designs merely expressed a universal and eternal law of nature:

> Of the gods we believe, and of men we know, that by a necessary law of nature they rule wherever they can. And it is not as if we were the first to make this law, or to act upon it when made: We found it existing before us, and we shall leave it to exist forever after us; all we do is make use of it, knowing that you and everybody else, having the same power as we have, would do the same as we do.

Thucydides' *History* offers the most powerful permutations of the sinister nature-fragile culture dualism, since he was able to formulate the relationship in many different ways, including several ways that contradicted one another. Or else, when the resort to human nature proved inconvenient, he forgot about it. With regard to the law of rule-by-those-who-can in the "Melian Dialogue," he seems to have forgotten the important passage in Book I where he has the Corinthians remonstrating with their Spartan allies for not acting like the domineering Athenians, although they have the same power to do so. Indeed, unlike the Athenians, who are ambitious for power even beyond their means, the Spartans habitually attempt less in this regard than they could accomplish. This passage is a critical one in Thucydides' text because it sets out the temperamental differences between the Spartans and Athenians that help explain their differences in foreign policy and military strategy—from which one could conclude that in more ways than one the Spartans were human-nature challenged.

Then again, the natural will to power itself has some contradictory effects, inasmuch as Thucydides made it responsible both for the revolution at Corcyra and Athenian imperialism: in the first case, he says the desire of power "was the enemy to all superiority," if in the second it was the motivation thereof. Yet this is only one of several such instances in which human nature is here the maker of culture and there the breaker. In still another *nomos-physis* permutation, Thucydides sees culture functioning as a beneficent disguise of a self-interested human nature ever ready to break out in destructive fury. The civil war in Corcyra was the first of many such conflicts whose causes lie in men's "lust for power arising from greed and ambition;" yet the leaders of these conflicts "sought prizes for themselves in those public interests which they pretended to cherish," even as they wrought disorder under "the fairest professions: on one side with the cry of political equality of the people, on the other of a moderate aristocracy." So culture is either the social form of natural impulses, or when it is not, when the city is organized on principles of justice, morality, equality and other such fair names, this is only a superficial mystification of a truer and stronger human nature. In a debate in the Athenian assembly over the fate of the rebel city of Mytilene, one Diodotus observes: "In short, it is impossible to prevent, and only great simplicity can hope to prevent, human nature doing what it has once set its mind upon, by force of law or any other deterrent whatever."

Yes, whatever: human nature as order or disorder, the cultural form or its natural antithesis, manifest or mystified, it's all human nature. This is a no-loss historiography in which it is only human nature to act contrary to human nature—thus making human nature the unbeatable heavyweight champion of world history.

It reigns still in American imperial designs on world history, only that the inherent self-concern that would be thus propagated has been revalued as "individual freedom." Otherwise, the American project of neo-liberal democracy for everyone operates on the same ancient premise of the superficiality of culture and its vulnerability to man's natural acquisitiveness—as enforced by the rule of the strongest. What was the line in *Full Metal Jacket*, the film about the Vietnam War? Something like, "Inside every gook, there's an American waiting to come out." The presumption is that the innate self concern—a.k.a., "desire for freedom"—common to humanity, if it can be relieved of local cultural idiosyncrasies, if necessary by applying the kind of force anyone can understand, will make other peoples happy and good just like us. In a recent book on the Iraq War, George Packer, commenting on the famous response of the then U.S. Secretary of Defense to the post-conquest looting of the country, viz., "stuff happens," makes Mr. Rumsfeld out to be a perfect sophist:

> Rumsfeld's words, which soon became notorious, implied a whole political philosophy. The defense secretary looked upon anarchy and saw the early stages of democracy. In his view and that of others in the administration, freedom was the absence of constraint. Freedom existed in divinely endowed human nature, not in man-made institutions and laws. Remove a thirty-five-year-old tyranny and democracy will grow in its place, because people everywhere want to be free.

Alternative Concepts of the Human Condition

Perhaps the antithesis of nature (*physis*) and culture (*nomos*) became an issue with the origin of the state and its encroachments on the "natural" bonds of kinship—although the question would remain, why in Greece and not in many other societies that experienced the same development? In any case, it seems fair to say that the dramatic conflicts between kinship and the city that since Homer were a revisited topos of the poets involved just such reflections on the nature-culture divide. In Sophocles' *Antigone*, tragedy inheres in the incompatibilities between the principles of the kindred and the prescriptions of the polis, as personified in Antigone's defiance of Creon, tyrant ruler of Thebes. By forbidding her to bury her brother because he was an enemy of the city, having died in an attack upon it, Creon put the laws of the state before Antigone's obligation to her kinsman. Creon is intransigent, but only until he becomes a victim of the same opposition, when his civic policy makes a mortal victim of his own son. For present purposes, the moral may be something more than another good nature/bad culture variant of the ancient dualism. The argument from familial obligation involves conceptions of the human condition undreamed of in our received philosophies of human nature, for what means "self-interest" when both selves and interests are transpersonal relationships rather than predicates of individuals?

Beyond the current controversies over human nature and its supposed cultural complements, the Western tradition has long harbored an alternative conception of order and being, of the kind anthropologists have often studied: kinship community. True that in the West this is the unmarked human condition, despite that (or perhaps because) family and kindred relations are sources of our deepest sentiments and attachments. Ignoring these, our philosophies of human nature generally come from the larger society, organized on radically different principles. What we are pleased to consider human nature mostly consists of the inclinations of (bourgeois) adult males, largely to the exclusion of women, children and old folks and to the comparative neglect of the one universal principle of human sociality, kinship. One would think that human nature begins at home; but then it would have to be understood differently than self-interest, since charity was always already there.

The lurking contradiction may help account for some remarkable recommendations of kinship community and subjectivity on the part of the ancients. Plato and Augustine both formulated a broad system of Hawaiian-type kinship as the mode of society most appropriate for mankind: Augustine asserting that this conception of humanity as family was the original, divinely-ordained social order; Plato, that it was the ideal civil society among the enlightened classes of his utopian Republic. In Hawaiian systems everyone is related to everyone in the community through the primary ties of mother, father, brother, sister, son and daughter. It was not for nothing, opined Augustine, but rather for universal love that God made us descendants of a single ancestor, thus all mankind but one kindred. The Bishop of Hippo also forestalled E.B. Tylor's famous explanation of the incest taboo—"marry out or die out"—by some fifteen hundred years, arguing that the prohibition of unions within the family would multiply the number of its kindred relations and accordingly broaden its support. (One would have a sister, a wife and in-laws rather than a sister who is a wife and one's natal family only.) Speaking thus of the community of common ancestry, the encompassment of distant kin in primary relationships (classificatory kinship), the incest taboo and marrying out (exogamy), these ancient anthropologies could already perceive kinship as a collective order.

Still it was Aristotle in the *Nichomachean Ethics* who penned what still seems the best determination of what kinship is. Reading Aristotle on the friendship of kinsmen, one could be reading Marilyn Strathern (on the New Guinea Highlands) or Janet Carsten (on Indonesian islanders) analyzing kinship as relationships to others intrinsic to a person's subjective being and objective identity. Just so for Aristotle, kinsmen are the same entity in different subjects; children are their parents' other selves; and brothers, cousins and other relatives are people who belong to one another, if in varying degrees:

> Parents then love children as being themselves (for those sprung from them are as it were other selves of theirs, resulting from the separation), children love parents as being what they have grown from, and brothers each other by virtue of their having grown from the same sources: for the self-sameness of their relation to those produces the same with each other (hence people say 'same blood,' 'same root,' and things like that). They are, then, the same entity in a way, even though in different subjects....The belong-ing to each other of cousins and other relatives derives from these, since it exists by virtue of their being from the same origins, but some of these

belong more closely while others are more distant, depending on whether the ancestral common sources are near or far off. (*Nich. Eth. 1162a*).

If I may be allowed to abstract the general principle, kinship is a mutual relationship of being. Kinsmen are members of one another. Their mutuality may be a sameness of being, as among brothers or descendants of a common ancestor; or it may entail belonging to one another in a reciprocal and complementary relationship, as between husband and wife. In any case, the relationship to the other, and in that sense the other himself or herself, is intrinsic to one's own existence.

Aristotle spoke primarily of the kinship of sameness, the one entity in different subjects, as engendered by birth and descent and objectified by shared bodily substance; thus people of the "same blood" or the same stock. Yet in giving salience only to the kinship of the same kind or common descent, Aristotle's concept of relatedness was incomplete. It was an early reflection of the long-standing Western distinction between the naturalness of kinship by birth or by "blood" in contrast to man-made relationships by marriage or by law: the self-same opposition of *physis* and *nomos* that David Schneider discerned in a celebrated study of modern American kinship. Still this privilege given to consanguinity is not a necessary bias of kinship everywhere, or even of the definition of the in-group of "same people." Ethnographers tell of people who establish a solidary kinship of sameness on various principles, including common residence, common history, common land rights, gift exchange, food-providing and shared memories, among other ways of thus constituting mutuality of being. It would hardly need saying, except for sociobiological delusions on this score, that the determination of kin relationships is not necessarily genealogical and need not entail any sense of the corporeal identity of those known as relatives: no necessity of shared substance at all. What is, however, universally valid in Aristotle's description of kinship as the one entity in different subjects is the ethics of this sameness: the love such kinsmen are enjoined to have for one another. In respect of their common identity they are equals, although they may be differentiated in other ways, and the generic economic relation among them should be mutual aid. "Kinship" and "kindness" E.B. Tylor once observed, have a common root, a derivation that expresses in the happiest way one of the main principles of social life.

Yet for all its ethics of love and mutual aid, a kinship group of the "same people" or "own people" cannot reproduce itself, inasmuch as the incest taboo deprives it of necessary generative capacities and enjoins its dependence on the external others who supply the want. The marital exchanges that transfer members of one group into the households of others effect a circulation of life powers, thus constituting vital kinship relations of difference, alliances with others that create children as complementary beings. (These transfers usually involve the reproductive contributions of men in matrilineal orders, of women in patrilineal, or of either in other kinship schemes.) The affinal relationship is thus a real-life, experiential form of the great mystical predicament of the human condition: that people truly depend on *sui generis* powers of vitality and mortality of which they are neither the authors or the masters, powers rather that exist outside their own self-organized communities. If people did control their own existence, they would not die. Nor do they control the elements, the seasons, or other such conditions on which their welfare depends. Hence the frequent and widely-distributed ethnographic reports that link affinal relatives to cosmic beings that govern the human fate, for the former are likewise life-giving or life-taking through the transactions of marriage. Even important gods may be affines, and important affines gods. Hence also, as Edmund Leach famously observed, "relations of alliance are viewed as metaphysical influence." Blessings and curses pass through affinal bonds. Here, in kinship, as in relations to the cosmos in general, alterity is a condition of the possibility of being.

Ethnographic reports speak of "the transpersonal self" (Native Americans), of the self as "a locus of shared social relations or shared biographies"(Caroline Islands), of persons as "the plural and composite site of the relationships that produced them" (New Guinea Highlands). Referring broadly to the African concept of "the individual," Roger Bastide writes: "He does not exist except to the extent he is 'outside' and 'different' from himself." Clearly the self in these societies is not synonymous with the bounded, unitary and autonomous individual as we know him— *him* in particular, as in our social theory if not our kinship practice. Rather, the individual person is the locus of multiple other selves with whom he or she is joined in mutual relations of being; even as, for the same reason, any person's self is more or less widely distributed among others. McKim Marriott's notice of this phenomenon in India first brought it to anthropological attention:

Persons—single actors—are not thought in South Asia to be "individual," that is, indivisible bounded units, as they are in much of Western social and psychological theory as well as in common sense. Instead, it appears that persons are generally thought of by South Asians to be "dividual" or divisible. To exist, dividual persons absorb heterogeneous material influences. They must also give out from themselves particles of their own coded substances—essences, residues or other active influence—they may then reproduce in others something of the nature of the persons in whom they have originated.

In sum and in general, in kin relationships, others become predicates of one's own existence and vice versa. I do not mean the interchange of standpoints that is a feature of all direct social relationships according to the phenomenologists. I do mean the integration of certain relationships, hence the participation of certain others in one's own being. And if "I am another," then the other is also my own purpose.

As members of one another, kinsmen lead each other's lives and die each other's deaths. One works and acts in terms of relationships, with others in mind, thus on behalf of one's child, cross-cousin, husband, clansmen, mothers' brother, or other kinsperson. In this regard, Marilyn Strathern observes of New Guinea peoples, neither agency nor intentionality is a simple expression of individuality, inasmuch the being of the other is an internal condition of one's own activity. Not only work but consumption itself is "no simple matter of self-replacement," Strathern notes, "but the recognition and monitoring of relationships." Unlike the classic bourgeois individualism, the body is not the private possession of the individual. "A body is the responsibility of the micro-community that feeds and cares for it," Anne Becker reports of Fijian people; "consequently, crafting its form is the province of the community rather than the self." The body's shape is a matter of village comment and concern, since it encodes the community's ability to care for its members and the individual's capacity to serve others. In such kinship communities, the body is a social body, the subject of the empathy, concern and responsibility of others, as it is also and reciprocally devoted to their well-being.

It follows that neither is experience an exclusively individual function. In the manner and to the extent that people are members of one another, so may experiences be shared among them. Not at the level of sensation, of course, but at the level of meaning: of what it is that happens, which is the human cum communicable quality of experience. "Experience was diffused among persons," Maurice Lienhardt told of New Caledonians, "it was not considered specific to the individual." People suffered illnesses as a result of moral or religious transgressions of their relatives—a common ethnographic finding. Many are the societies where kinsmen must be compensated for the injuries one receives, even more for one's death, although something less for having one's hair cut. In many also, the affinal kin of the injured or deceased have a special right of compensation, because they are the source of the life concerned. Thus this notice of the Northeast Coast Tlingit:

> Perceived as being closely connected to each other, all clan members are affected whenever one of them was insulted or hurt physically, not to mention his death. If a clan member injured himself, he not only had to give a feast and offer gifts to the "opposite

side" [that is, affines of the opposite moiety], but was expected to sponsor a small feast for his own clan for the embarrassment brought upon them by his disfigurement.

Numerous again are the societies where people die symbolically with their relatives: not only by self-inflicted wounds, but as removed from society by mourning practices that negate their normal social personhood: seclusion, torn apparel, interdiction on bathing and the like. Not to claim these practices are universal; but often enough people do not die alone. Death too is a shared fact.

Natural self-interest? For the greater part of humanity, self-interest as we know it is unnatural in the normative sense: it is considered madness, witchcraft or some such grounds for ostracism, execution or at least therapy. Rather than expressing a pre-social human nature, such avarice is generally taken for a loss of humanity. It puts in abeyance the mutual relationships of being that define a human existence. Yet if the self, the body, experience, pleasure, pain, agency and intentionality, even death itself, are transpersonal relationships in so many societies, and in all likelihood through so many eons of human history, it follows that the native Western concept of man's self-regarding animal nature is an illusion of world-anthropological proportions.

Medieval Monarchy

In a line of thought that stretches from the theology of St. Augustine to the sociology of Emile Durkheim, society is conditional on the worst in us. Through the Middle Ages into modern times, society has regularly been viewed as a necessary and coercive antidote for our inherent egoism. This wickedness, moreover, is humankind's own doing. Paul Riceour makes a point of the singularity of the Western cosmogony in which evil was neither a primordial condition nor a divinely orchestrated tragedy but uniquely the responsibility of man, self-loving man, who disobeyed God to please himself. Eve and the devilish serpent had a hand in it, but Adam has had to take the blame. Moreover, since the seed was transmitted in Adam's semen, as St. Augustine supposed, it follows that "we are all in that one man." So whatever the differences among the Ancients about humans' innate character, Original Sin pretty much sealed the deal in Christendom for centuries to come. Augustine's influential concept of Original Sin, observes Elaine Pagels, "offered an analysis of human nature that became, for better and worse, the heritage of all subsequent generations of Western Christians and a major influence on their psychological and political thinking." The big effect on political thinking was a broad consensus on the functionality of government in general, monarchy in particular, in repressing human savagery.

Otherwise, people would devour each other like fishes or other wild beasts. Endless desires of the flesh would lead to endless war: within men, between men and with Nature. "How they mutually oppress," said

Augustine, "and how they that are able do devour, and when one fish hath devoured, the greater the less, itself is also devoured by another." Iranaeus' vision of the fish story was already derived from an older rabbinical tradition: "Earthly rule has been appointed by God for the benefit of nations, so that under fear of human rule, men may not devour each other like fishes." As a totemic model of human nature, big fish eating little fish remained proverbial throughout the Middle Ages and it still does service as a trenchant description of neo-liberal capitalism. (Some years back, a toy Christmas gift of the same description was marketed especially for corporate executives.) The companion idea that people are even worse to each other than beasts—"not even lions or tigers," it says in *The City of God*, "have ever waged war with their kind as men have waged war with one another"—has also been the stuff of Christian fable about the necessity of earthly authority. "If you deprive the city of its rulers, we would live a life less rational than animals, biting and devouring each other." (John Chrysostum.) The city: not to forget that Cain founded the first city. He was the fratricidal first-born son of the incestuous union of Adam and Eve; and he populated his city by bedding an unnamed woman who must have been his sister, if she was not his mother.

Where law governs, the city is ruled by reason and God, Aristotle said, but to have men govern "adds a wild animal also; for appetite is like a wild animal, and passion warps the rule of the best men." Augustine too had reservations about the licensed brigandage of the state, but for all that, it was the institutionalized violence exercised by the powers-that-be that made them indispensable to fallen humanity. Augustine could thus endorse not only the powers of the king, but the death penalty of the judge, the barbed hook of the executioner, the weapons of the soldier and even the severity of the good father. "While all these are feared," he concluded, "the wicked are kept within bounds and the good live peacefully among the wicked."

Medievalists call this politics of Original Sin *political Augustinism*. Rule from above and beyond, over and against the evilly-inclined underlying population was the general principle, applicable to the feudal lord as well as the emperor or king, and to the bishop as well as the pope. Ideally, it was also a hierarchy of virtue in which the majesty and power of those in command, "the good people" (*le bons gens*), was potentiated by their ability to restrain their own appetites. The control of their own bestiality allowed them to control the villainy of lower orders, where Original Sin and brutality were particularly sedimented—to erupt periodically in Rabelaisian rituals of the "material bodily lower stratum." In a work on *The Political and Social Ideas of St. Augustine*, Herbert Deane makes a sustained comparison to Thomas Hobbes' similar thesis of royal power as a bridle to man's selfish and destructive impulses. So it should not be surprising that in speaking of the Christianized version of majesty-against-savagery, Henry Chadwick invokes Thucydides' description of "the hell of anarchy"—which has to be a reference to the *stasis* at Corcyra:

> It is certain from St. Paul's words that "the magistrate does not bear the sword to no purpose," that because of the cupidity and pride in the heart of fallen man, a power of coercion is an indispensable restraint. The magistrate will get no one to heaven, but he may yet do something to fence the broad

road to the hell of anarchy which, as Thucydides observed with disturbing eloquence, brings out the full human capacity for depravity.

As a providential remedy for anarchy, medieval majesty had a certain affinity with divinity. It is said of H.R.E. Frederick II (1411-1464)—by Ernst Kantorowicz in *The King's Two Bodies*—a monarch "who like every Medieval ruler claimed also to be the vice-regent of God," that he comforted himself with the thought that as the arbiter of the life and death of his people, he was the executor of Divine Providence. Besides the vice-regent of God, the king could be His vicar, His successor on earth or the Christ-like god-man. The king's mortal frame was the temporary abode of the immortal power reigning over the human realm, hence the Christological aspect of his dual personage. The high medieval ruler became *christomimétés*, the "actor" or "impersonator" of Christ. Such was his personage by consecration and by grace, as in the text (c. 1100) of the Norman Anonymous provided by Kantorowicz:

> The power of the king is the power of God. This power, namely, is God's by nature, and the king's by grace. Hence the king, too, is God and Christ, but by grace; and whatsoever he does, he does not simply as a man, but as one who has become God by grace.

The mid-twelfth century political treatise of John of Salisbury spoke of the ruling prince as "a certain image on earth of the divine majesty." One could know this by how dreaded was the king. People would not bow their heads to the ruler's nod or their necks to the sacrificial axe, Salisbury said, were it not that "by divine impulse everyone fears him who is fear itself." The complementary aspect of coercive rule is universal fear, already known in Augustine and brilliantly rehearsed in Hobbes' theory of the contract, where in effect every man exchanges his private fear of a violent death for a collective fear that will secure a general peace.

In John of Salisbury's treatment, as also in the politcs of Dante, Aquinas, John of Paris, Giles of Rome and other intellectual worthies, monarchy was a whole cosmology. Or then again, it was a general metaphysics of order based on the derivation of the inferior Many from the superior One. Adapting the Aristotelian system of the universe to Christian doctrine, Dante in his text on world monarchy argued that, "since the whole sphere of heaven is guided by a single movement (i.e., that of the *Primum Mobile*), and by a single source of motion (who is God), in all parts, movements and causes of movement," so then "mankind is in an ideal state when it is guided by a single ruler (as by a single source of motion) and in accordance with a single law." Dante also put to monarchial service a popular distinction Aristotle had made in the *Metaphysics* between two different modes of ordering the good, which is also to say, of good order. One is the order established by the reciprocal relations of parts within a whole, as between soldiers in an army. The other is the good emanating from the purpose and plan of an external authority, the way a general is responsible for the order of the army as a whole. At the end of the relevant book on the *Metaphysics*, Aristotle observed that "things do not wish to be governed badly," to which he appended the endorsement of Agamemnon's supremacy in *The Iliad*: "The rule of many is not good; let one the ruler be."

I am uncertain whether these contrasting forms of order were originally meant to be abstract forms of the opposition between hierarchical and egalitarian regimes of the kind being discussed here. But when this Aristotelian distinction was coupled to his contrast of distributive and commutative (or rectificatory) justice by Aquinas, and especially by Aquinas' disciple Giles of Rome, then clearly we have to do with abstract statements of monarchial and republican order. For where distributive justice consists of the bestowal of value from the center to the many in proportion to rank, commutative justice involves reparations that restore the equality of one party to another. Indeed the latter was described by Giles of Rome in a way reminiscent of the cosmic justice of Anaximander, which had likewise involved reparations for incursions of bodies on their equals. As for Dante, he thought the monarchial form best, not only because the dominant entity embodied the purpose of the whole, but because the relationship between parts of the whole was dependent on their mutual subordination to the external rule. In more pragmatic terms, Dante's *Monarchia* was an argument for universal kingship on the usual ground of the neutralization of human cupidity: men would scatter like horses if they were not thus controlled "by bit and bridle."

Nor should old Aquinas be forgot, then, when it comes to the metaphysics of monarchy. In his own treatise on kingship, Aquinas found monarchy everywhere on earth, as it was in heaven, on the proposition that whenever things are organized in a unity there is always something that rules the rest. All bodies in the cosmos are ruled by one primary celestial body; all earthly bodies are ruled by rational creatures; in man, the body is ruled by the soul; in the soul, the irascible and concupiscible appetites are ruled by reason; while within the body proper, the members are ruled by the head or the heart—hence it is fitting that "in every multitude there should be a ruling principle." And having noted a few paragraphs on that even bees have a king (*sic*), St. Thomas concluded that all multiplicity is derived from unity.

There was a prince in everything. The derivation of the Many from the One ran from the whole animated by God through the earthly lordships to the least of things, in a series of progressive segmentation and decreasing value, each part being in its own organization a replica of the higher entity that included it. The same principle prevailed down to the compounds of inanimate matter: "in the whole of inanimate nature," Otto Gierke has observed, "we shall find no compound substance in which there is not one element which determines the nature of the whole." The monarchial chain of being thereby composed a matrix of reciprocal analogues, available for the many routine depictions of the Lord as sovereign and the sovereign as Lord, the kingdom as a human body and the body as a kingdom, etc. Wycliffe offered an Aristotelian alternative: "In polity, the people are the matter and the king is the form" —an apt rendering of the king as ordering principle, though it carried the non-Aristotelian implication that people were by nature without order.

Aristotle held that by nature people live in political societies—that man was a political animal—an idea that from the thirteenth century Aquinas and followers proceeded to develop against the grain of the going Augustinism. If mankind were naturally social, it would relieve the stigma of Original Sin, making its remedy of coercive rule unnecessary and offering some hope of felicity in an earthly life that for Augustine was a vale of tears. Yet as we know, there was a pervasive contradiction in Aristotle's natural sociality, something like a *nomos-physis* opposition that tended to undermine it—and that Aquinas' version made rather worse. For although man's rational soul was naturally inclined to curb base desires, Aristotle argued that it had to be trained up to do so; whereas, the appetitive soul was of itself and spontaneously insatiable. "Appetite is by nature unlimited," he wrote in the *Politics*, "and the majority of mankind live for the satisfaction of appetite." Hence men may be social by nature, but apparently they are not naturally sociable. Here was an opening for Aquinas' introduction of interest and need as a basis of society—from which followed a certain recuperation of kingship as a necessary instrument of community.

St. Thomas largely resolved Aristotle's dictum that man is a political animal to an economic function, stressing that people's association in the *polis* was the necessary means of their material existence. Aristotle had explicitly denied that the *polis* was formed for any particular or immediate advantage, but only for the all round good lives of the citizens. However, for Aquinas (and followers such as John of Paris), society was natural in the sense that only by congregating in sufficient numbers might people gain their livelihood. Neither alone nor in families could they fend for themselves. The city alone could provide the requisite population, skills and division of labor. Paradoxically, St. Thomas would thus realize an Aristotelian condition of the good—i.e., self-sufficiency or completeness, which is indeed a human version of divinity—by installing need, desire and interest in the formation of society—which is also to say, by Original Sin, more or less naturalized. (This idea that society originates in material need remains current in the Social Sciences of our day, as it was famously among Helvétius, Baron d' Holbach and other Enlightenment materialists.) In Aquinas' formulation, then, the original social condition was in effect a petty bourgeoisdom consisting of independent producers each looking out for their own good while dependent on exchange with each other. Absent an external authority, the arrangement did not bode well. Following Aristotle, St. Thomas too thought that "the desire to seek their own good is present in the souls of all men;" and further that "those who have riches will desire to have more," and no earthly thing will pacify them. What they needed was a king whose virtue could transcend the self-concern of his subjects and allow him to reconcile their conflicts in the common interest. "For if many men were to live together with each providing only what is convenient for himself, the community would break up into various parts unless one of them had the responsibility for the good of the community as a whole." By the naturalization of Original Sin in the form of material self-interest, St. Thomas motivates an ideology of kingship that, in the larger view, looks like a more-or-less benign form of political Augustinism.

This helps explain why the philosopher Alan Gewirth finds a significant resemblance between the politics of Aquinas and—guess who?—Thomas Hobbes.

St. Thomas was known to meliorate his support of kingship by advocating some distribution of its powers among the grandees and the people, as in

Polybian mixed government. But in time the monarchial order increasingly suffered its own contradictions. Liberty, contract, representation and consent of the governed were known in some form in feudalism itself. Kingship gradually lost its externality, its claim to be above and beyond society, to become instead society's instrument and subject to its laws. Add the doctrine that the king ruled by delegation from the people, and the determination of who was the sovereign power was up for grabs—especially as it could be debated that the people's consent was not a definitive abdication. Then, there was the developing autonomy of cities, guilds and peasant communes. Marc Bloch tells of the long and sometimes violent struggles of the peasants for self-government that began in the ninth century. Inspired by movements toward autonomy in many towns during the eleventh century wherein the burgesses joined in oaths of mutual aid, the peasants developed a certain preoccupation with the "primitive egalitarianism" of the Gospels. Indeed all such compromises of lordship could find encouragement and support in the critical negation lurking in medieval Christendom from the beginning: from the Garden of Eden and the Scriptures, with their vision of the original equality of humankind in the sight of God and their community in the body of Christ.

From the Church Fathers to the Scholastics, the consensus of doctrinal opinion held it was only after the Fall that humanity was forced to submit to coercive government, private property, inequality in general and kingship and slavery in particular. Implemented by men, if sanctioned by God, all these were devised to control human wickedness—or as Thomas Gilby put it, "to make the best of a bad lot." But then, as Gilby also observed, the opposition between the equality of man's original nature and the institutions of his fallen state (or second nature) was overlaid by the ancient distinction between nature and convention, *physis* and *nomos*, thus endowing these institutions of medieval civilization with the invidious distinction of artificiality. "Human convention," said St. Thomas, "rather than Natural Law brings about the division of property." As largely man-made and morally devalued by comparison to the state of innocence, kingship was thus vulnerable to an egalitarian critique. This punitive institution was not what God originally intended when he made men free and equal. Which suggests that all along, inside the medieval regime of hierarchy there was a free, egalitarian republic waiting to come out.

Renaissance Republics

Beginning late in the 11th century, the egalitarian republic did get out in Pisa, Milan, Genoa, Lucca, Bologna, Florence and other cities of Lombardy and Tuscany. Whether persuaded they were naturally good as the Bible said, or capable of civic virtue as Cicero said, men no longer needed to think that God had sanctioned their subjection to princes in order to repress their wickedness. Men (only men) became active citizens prescribing laws for themselves rather than passive subjects suffering the authority imposed upon them. Quentin Skinner notes that many of the "prehumanists" engaged in philosophizing the state "treat it as a distinctive virtue of elective systems that they guarantee the equality of all citizens before the law. No one's interests are excluded, no one is unfairly subordinated to anyone else." When Aristotle's late medieval bestseller, the *Politics*, became available, this freedom from divinely-sanctioned monarchy could also be justified by arguments from man's innate civic nature; and certain cities could boast of following his ideal of a government where men rule and are ruled by turn, for their magistrates were salaried officials elected for short terms from the citizenry at large. By Florentine law of 1538, the city rulers were selected by lot, literally out of a bag, from all men in good standing.

In the early republics, however, the classical formulas of mixed government combining the rule of the few and the many were not usually regarded as systems of checks and balances. They were viewed rather as means of insuring class harmony in the Milo Minderbinder principle (in *Catch 22*) of "everyone has a share." The idea was that if everyone had a share in government, no one would be tempted to rebel. Civic peace was indeed an obsession because it was constantly threatened, and the judicial systems proved unable to protect the interests of all. As against the various partisan interests, the collective interest of the city was largely confined to preaching professors of the civic virtues of the old Roman Republic. One might consider this the Orphic solution to the recurrent problem of ensuring the public good while allowing the parties and persons of the city to pursue their own. Thomas Gustafson speaks of a revival of Ciceronian oratory: what "the humanists reclaim for eloquence and letters," he says, "is nothing less than the Orphic power to civilize or the God-like power to bring order out of chaos." Orpheus could tame the savage beasts by the sound of his voice and his lyre, but the problem was, as Cicero lamented of his own time, that "some belong to a democratic party, others to an aristocratic party, but few to a national party." So it was in many of the Italian republics. Skinner cites the prehumanist Giovanni da Viterbo: "there is scarcely a city to be found anywhere that is not divided against itself." Fallen into factional discord, most of the cities that had become republics by the mid-12th century lapsed and again put their trust in princes by the end of the thirteenth.

The Florentine republic managed to survive (fitfully) into the sixteenth century—perhaps in part by a structural process of complementary opposition to rival cities that were more hierarchically organized. Indeed where many intellectuals in other cities had conveniently switched over to the mirror-for-princes business, Leonardo Bruni (1370-1444), longtime chancellor of Florence and greatest civic humanist of his time, was an enemy of the Caesarism that had over-taken other republics and was coming on in his own. Bruni was a party to the revision of Florence's traditional origin myth from a camp of Caesar's soldiers to an earlier, republican settlement of Romans whose sense of liberty was fortified by the incorporation of survivors from the autonomous Etruscan cities that preceded them. As an orator, a republican and a Florentine patriot, Bruni was a rare Ciceronian exemplar of effective partisan of the collective interest. This, for instance, from the *Oration for the Funeral of Nanni Strozzi*:

> The constitution we use for the government of the republic is designed for the liberty and equality of indeed all the citizens....We do not tremble beneath the rule of one man who would lord it over us, nor are we slaves to the rule of a few. Our liberty is equal for all; it is limited only by the laws, and is free from the fear of man. The hope of attaining office and of raising oneself up is the same for all...Virtue and probity are required of the citizens by our city. Anyone who has these two qualities is thought to be sufficiently well-born to govern the republic.

Bruni knew that the stability of the republic depended on more than equality in principle (*isonomia*). In his *Panegyric to the City of Florence*, he notes also: "we have succeeded in *balancing* all the sections of our city in such a way as to produce harmony in every aspect of the Republic" (my emphasis). The Florentine republic survives not by avoiding the clash of interests that brought down republicanism in other cities but by institutionalizing it. Yet it was Machiavelli who most famously made a virtue of self-seeking strife as a constitutional means of transforming factionalism into fortune and freedom.

It was up to Machiavelli to "get real" about civic virtue. I use the expression because so many describe Machiavelli's discourse as "realism," that is, in reference to his sophistic imaginary that, at least in crisis, man's darker nature should prevail over justice and morality. Not only in *The Prince* but in his republican persona in *The Discourses on Livy*, Machiavelli radically subverted the earlier faith in civic peace as the necessary condition of civic greatness. The heading of Chapter 4, Book 1 of *The Discourses* reads: "The Discord between the Plebs and the Senate of Rome made this Republic both Free and Powerful." People who cavil at these conflicts, he said, are paying too much attention to the tumults and not enough to the liberty they produced. Republics everywhere, he said, are beset with the opposition between the popular and privileged classes, "and all legislation favorable to liberty is brought about by the clash between them." Although the "Machiavellian moment," as J.G.A. Pocock famously set forth, introduces a new temporality of contingency and change in human affairs, upsetting the eternal, divinely ordered universe of the received Christian wisdom, there remained an essential continuity: that sempiternal figure of self-pleasing man, whom Machiavelli regarded as an inevitable political condition.

Even in *The Prince*, the basic motivation of the shifty morality Machiavelli recommends for rulers is the yet more consistent immorality of their subjects. Only by their own duplicity can princes contend with men of whom one can take it as a general rule that "they are ungrateful, fickle, liars and deceivers, fearful of danger and greedy for gain." (Machiavelli's compatriot, Francesco Guicciardini offered similar advice on the same basis: "The wickedness of man is such that you cannot govern without severity. But you must be clever about it.") Again in *The Discourses* Machiavelli says,

> All writers on politics have pointed out, and throughout history there are plenty of examples which indicate, that in constituting and legislating for a commonwealth, it must needs be taken for granted that all men are wicked, and that they will always give vent to the malignity that is in their minds when the opportunity offers.

But in this republican context such malignant self-concern can have positive functions. Machiavelli claimed that allowing the free play of factional interests could even answer the ancient question of how then to establish the common interest—though his answer rather begged the question. Good examples of civic virtue will come from good education, he said, good education from good laws, "and good laws from those very tumults which so many condemn." Yes but how do good laws come from tumults of self-interest—most of which, as Pocock points out, have merely the negative character of the plebs resisting the patricians' attempts at domination?

Still, the coherence of the whole that self-regulating contentiousness could not achieve in the Renaissance republic it managed produce in the larger scale of the cosmos. In a work entitled *The Nature of Things According to Their Own Proper Principles* (1565), Bernardino Telesio of Cosenza generalized self-interest into a universal principle of natural dynamics and cosmic organization. Telesio proves that if Anaximander hadn't lived, the Renaissance would have had to invent him. "It is quite evident," he wrote, "that nature is propelled by self-interest." As in Anaximander's universe, in Telesio's all things are produced through the interaction of opposed elementary qualities—here Heat and Cold emanating from the Sun and the Earth—and the bodies thus composed invade one another in their self-interested attempts to realize their own being. For all entities, animate and inanimate, are endowed with sensory capacities, and they react to other things in terms of pleasure and pain in order to grow themselves. "It is not blind and senseless chance, then, that brings active natures into perpetual conflict. They all desire in the highest degree to preserve themselves: they strive, furthermore, to grow and reproduce their individual subjects…"

Unlike Anaximander, however, Telesio sees no reconciliation of these conflicts by a sense of justice. Virtue comes down to the bedrock self-aggrandizement that makes a self-organized world. If the world is then organized, it is as if by an Invisible Hand—of which concept Telesio was one of the first to give a political, ethical and natural expression, according to Amos Funkenstein. But aside from the fact that Anaximander beat him to it by 2000 years (plus), it is perhaps evident that Invisible Hand doctrines are normally formed in regimes of many kinds—political, economic, cosmological or corporeal—that are founded on the opposition of self-interested parties. Otherwise, in a politics of this genre, the melding of private interests with the collective good seems most likely under the contingent circumstances of an external military threat. Absent external competition, however, one must rely on the uncertain tactic of conceding the interests of others as the best way of defending one's own:

> So derives Self-love, thro' just and thro' unjust,
> To one Man's pow'r, ambition, lucre, lust:
> The same self-love, in all, becomes the cause
> Of what restrains him, Government and Laws. . . .
> 'Til' jarring int'rests of themselves create
> Th' according music of a well-mix'd State.
>
> (Alexander Pope, *Essay on Man*)

Before Pope, however, the English Renaissance had produced striking formulations of the alternative, monarchial resolution of jarring interests—including better poetry. If Telesio's self-regulating universe was reminiscent of Anaximander's, the Elizabethan world picture, as E.M.W. Tillyard described it, invoked a hier-archical, Aristotelian cosmos:

> It was a serious matter not a mere fancy if an Elizabethan writer compared Elizabeth to the primum mobile, the master sphere of the Universe, and every activity within the realm to the varied motions of the other spheres governed to the least fraction by the influence of their container.

But the long speech of Ulysses in Shakespeare's *Troilus and Cressida* (I. 3) detailing the disorders that would arise in society as in the cosmos from the clash of oppugnant powers, unless they were checked by hier-archical order and monarchial rule, is a golden example of the thesis of the present work. Reminiscent for its part of Thucydides on *stasis* for it evocation of under-lying evil and out-of-control disorder, lust of power, patricide, the right of might, the transgression of boundaries and even crooked words, the text has all the elements of the long Western nightmare of natural anarchy together with the politics of its resolution by sovereign authority. If I may be permitted, then, to quote at length:

> The heavens themselves, the planets, and this centre,
> Observe degree, priority and place,
> Insisture, course, proportion, season, form,
> Office, and custom, in all line of order;
> And, therefore, is the glorious planet Sol
> In noble eminence, enthroned and spher'd
> Amidst the others; whose medicinable eye
> Corrects the ill aspects of planets evil,
> And posts, like the commandment of a king,
> Sans cheque to good and bad: but when the planets
> In evil mixture to disorder wander,
> What plagues and what portents! What mutiny!
> What raging of the sea! Shaking of earth!
> Commotion in the winds, frights, changes, horrors,
> Divert and crack, rend and deracinate
> The unity and married calm of states
> Quite from their fixture! O, when degrees is shaked,
> Which is the ladder to all high designs,
> The enterprise is sick!...
> Take but degree away, untune that string,
> And, hark, what discord follows! each thing meets
> In mere oppugnancy: the bounded waters
> Should lift their bosoms higher than the shores,
> And make a sop of all this solid globe;
> Strength should be lord of imbecility,
> And the rude son should strike his father dead:
> Force should be right; or rather, right and wrong,
> Between whose endless jar justice resides,
> Should lose their names, and so should justice too.

Then every thing includes itself in power,
Power into will, will into appetite;
And appetite, an universal wolf,
So double seconded with will and power,
Must make perforce an universal prey
And last eat up himself.

Founding Fathers

On March 6, 1775, at the fifth anniversary commemoration of the Boston Tea party in the city's Old South Church, the orator of the day, Dr. Joseph Warren took the podium wearing a Roman toga. No doubt the audience knew how to understand Warren's sartorial intent, for they had already had considerable experience of this doubling of histories and identities among the leaders of the imminent American rebellion. Recall John Adams on Thucydides and Tacitus, "When I read them I seem to be only reading the History of my own Times and my own Life." Many of the Founders wrote under classical pseudonyms chosen to suit their politics or the occasion: the way that (speaking of Thucydides) Alexander Hamilton when arguing an attack on the French who had just taken over New Orleans signed himself "Pericles," in an allusion to the Athenian statesman's speech calling for war against Sparta. Regarding that ancient conflict, Thomas Jefferson presciently feared that disputes over slavery would eventually lead to an American reprise of the Peloponnesian War, with the commercial North taking the part of the Athenians against the helot-holding Spartans of the agrarian South. As Carl Richards wrote in his work on the Founders' relation to the classical tradition, for them, "the study of the past was not a mere antiquarian hobby. The past was alive with personal and social meaning. Their perception of that living past shaped their own identities."

What particularly shaped the Founders was their reading of the ancient civil wars of Greece and Rome and the horrors of human nature these conflicts seemed to reveal. In the same work in which he had taken up Thucydides' account of Corcyra, John Adams was at pains to rehearse the catalogue of massacres David Hume had collected from Diodorus of Sicily's *Library of History*. Speaking of the implications for America, Adams wrote: "Human nature is as incapable now of going through revolutions with temper and sobriety, with patience and prudence, or without fury and madness, as it was among the Greeks long ago." Hence Adams general historiographic stance on classical antiquity: "The history of Greece should be to our country now what is called by many families on the continent a boudoir; an octagonal apartment in a house with a full length mirror on every side and another on the ceiling." Standing there, Jefferson would have seen not only an all-round image of his American self but his vision of the similarity of the ancient class struggles and those now besetting the American republic. "The same political parties which now agitate the U.S. have existed through all time," he wrote. "Whether the power of the people or that of the *aristoi* should prevail kept Greece and Rome in eternal convulsions." ("Convulsions," recall, was Thucydides' word for it.) Likewise Alexander Hamilton (in *The Federalist* No.9):

> It is impossible to read the history of the petty republics of Greece and Italy without feeling sensations of horror and disgust at the distractions with which they were continually agitated, and at the rapid succession of revolutions by which they were kept in a perpetual vibration between the extremes of tyranny and anarchy.

The dismal view of human nature that the Founders could derive from ancient history was largely complemented by the Christian tradition of fallen man—if anything even more contemptible in the Calvinist version—and especially by its naturalized, Hobbesian recension. In general and in detail, James Madison's discussion (in *The Federalist* No.10) of the proposition that "The latent causes of faction are sown in the nature of man" harks back to Aristotle's sustained analysis of civil conflicts in Book V of the Politics (which also includes an allusion to the rebellion at Corcyra). Yet such contributions of the ancients notwithstanding, according to a long and distinguished historiographic tradition—which includes Richard Hofstadter, Robert Dahl, Horace White, and Charles Beard—the American republic was founded on the "pessimistic" or "jaundiced" sense of human nature that is usually and specifically characterized as "Hobbesian." (Another frequent characterization is "realist," thus ironically adding scholarly support to the Founders' illusion of human wickedness.) In an influential discussion of the same, Hofstadter endorses Horace White's observation that the United States was built on the philosophy of Hobbes and the religion of Calvin, which is to say, on the assumption that the natural state of humanity is war and the human mind is naturally at odds with the good. Although he gave no attribution, Madison (in *The Federalist* No.51) was evidently paying homage to Hobbes, notorious absolutist as he was, by paraphrasing his thesis on the origins of government:

> In a society under the forms of which the stronger faction can readily unite and oppress the weaker, anarchy may as truly be said to reign as in a state of

nature when the weaker individual is not secured against the violence of the stronger; and as, in the latter state, even the stronger individuals are prompted, by the uncertainty of their condition, to protect the weak as well as themselves: so in the former state, will the more powerful factions or parties be gradually induced, by like motive, to wish for a government that will protect all parties, the weaker as well as the more powerful.

Of course, rather than an absolute sovereign, Madison argued—in what turned out to be the most famous passage of *The Federalist Papers*—that

Ambition must be made to counteract ambition.... It may be a reflection of human nature that such devices should be necessary to control the abuses of government. But what is government itself but the greatest of all reflections on human nature? If men were angels, no government would be necessary.

Or in the equally famous words of Tom Paine in *Common Sense*, invoking the Christian rather than the Hobbesian condemnation of humankind: "Government, like dress, is the badge of lost innocence; the palaces of kings are built upon the ruins of the bowers of paradise." Paine also opined that, "Society is produced by our wants and government by our wickedness"—which rather neglected the common opinion that our wickedness is produced by our wants.

Common opinion: Hofstadter observed that to the Founders, "a human being was an atom of self-interest," and plenty of their statements bear him out. Whatever their disagreements about federal power and the protection of individual liberties, the Framers were generally operating on the dictum of Hamilton (taken from David Hume) that in "contriving any system of government, man ought to be supposed a knave." Argued Ben Franklin at the Federal Convention, "There are two passions which have a powerful influence in the affairs of men. These are ambition and avarice: the love of power and the love of money." A frequent refrain of the constitutional debates was the necessity to control human avarice and viciousness—which, moreover, could often be specifically located in the human breast. "To judge from the history of mankind," Hamilton wrote (in *The Federalist* No.34), "we shall be compelled to conclude that the fiery and destructive passions of war reign in the human breast with much more sway than the mild and beneficent sentiments of peace." Likewise John Lenoir in the North Carolina ratification debates: "We ought to consider the depravity of human nature, the predominant thirst for power which is in the breast of everyone." (Hey dude, whatever happened to the milk of human kindness?)

A lot of this so-called realism was being directed against the unruly masses by members of the possessing classes, who could agree with Madison (and John Locke) that the preservation of property was the first object of government. Here was the class opposition between the people and the *aristoi* that Jefferson had taken as something for the ages. Aside from the old landed proprietors, the American nouveau aristocracy included the commercial and financial grandees of the cities. Many of them had a healthy fear of the agitations of the poor against their wealth and privilege in the name of liberty, equality and democracy—known to them, however, as license or mob rule. The demands for the cancellation of debts (an issue leading to violence in the Shays Rebellion), the threats to property in populist state legislatures and the broad sentiments for its equal distribution, the rage for paper money: such "fury of democracy" had to be restrained, Edmund Randolph told the Constitutional Convention. For although it was generally acknowledged that the people were sovereign, it was also more or less conceded that they should not govern. On the contrary, they needed to be governed: as in the tripartite mixed government on Polybian lines favored by Adams and Hamilton where a "natural aristocracy" in the Senate, perhaps holding life terms, would keep the popular lower house in check. Some of the Founders, such as Gouverner Morris, were occasionally driven to think that only a monarchy would suffice. Still, this contradiction between popular sovereignty and democracy was only an aspect of the even larger contradiction between the Founders' fear of a naturally rapacious self-interest and their desire, as men of property and enterprise, to write it into the Constitution.

Their proposed resolution, of course, was the balance of oppugnant powers. To repeat John Adams' formulations: power must be opposed to power and interest to interest; passions, interests and power can be resisted only by passions, interests and power. The faith in the efficacy of the balance of powers was near to unconditional among the Founders, which is perhaps why its inscription in government was ever in contention, often indeterminate and sometimes completely illusory. In 1814, going onto three decades since the ratification of the Constitution, Adams catalogued eight different kinds of balance in that document, some of which were the well-known checks among the branches of government, others pitted the states against the federal government, the people against their representatives in biennial elections, the state legislatures against the Senate, and so forth. All of these, however, would be directed against tyranny in government, defending the population against state power, if not vice versa, but none actually responded to an ideal of mixed government in which party or class interest, as embodied for example in different branches of the legislature, opposed each other on equal terms.

In fact, since the Constitution proposed that the House, Senate and president were all to be elected directly or indirectly by the people, many of the delegates participating in the ratification debates already saw that the desired correspondence between governmental powers and classes wasn't happening. Dismayed by this failure, Patrick Henry spoke passionately at the Virginia convention against a Constitution that could forgo the one great check on political power: the self-love perpetuated from age to age in—where else?—every human breast:

> Tell me not of checks on paper; but tell me of checks founded on self-love. The English government is founded on self-love. This powerful irresistible stimulus of self-love has saved that government. It has interposed that hereditary nobility between the king and commons....Compare this with your Congressional checks. I beseech Gentlemen to consider, whether they can say, when trusting power, that a mere patriotic profession will be equally operative and efficacious, as the check of self-love....Where is the rock of your salvation? The real rock of political salvation is self-love, perpetuated from age to age in every human breast, and manifested in every action.

Recognizing that the Constitution had not provided the mixed government that Adams, Hamilton, Henry and others had wanted, James Madison argued that it still had the virtue of opposing interest to interest. Representation would lead to some such stand-off among estates. Farmers, financiers, manufacturers, tradesmen, etc., would be joined in stabilizing contention. The contention would work all the better, moreover, the larger the country and the more diverse the partisan interests, as region could then be played off against region and no one faction could gain the majority it needed to impose itself on the others. Expansion as the remedy for "the spirit of faction": this was one good argument for continental imperialism. Another was that expansion into the agrarian frontier would create a large cadre of middling yeomen—like Aristotle's idea of a predominant middle group—that by its weight could blunt the ambitions of the rich and the resentments of the poor. There was already abroad a notion that Americans by and large were equally fixed, just as today almost everyone is "middle class"—except for the nineteen percent of the population who think they are the upper one percent of annual income.

Still, the larger question remained of what virtue apart from self-love could support a commonwealth of self-love? What will sustain the common good? In one respect, the new republic was in a better position than its historic predecessor to address this issue insofar as self-interest had largely cast off its theological opprobrium. The problem seemed to find a solution of itself in the formula that we all have self-interest in the common interest as well as common interest in self-interest. By a rationalist interpretation such as David Hume's, men could be expected to voluntarily curb their own appetites in favor of collective well-being on pain of losing everything by a descent into anarchy. (Man's avidity of acquiring goods, said Hume, is "insatiable, perpetual, universal" and destructive of society—which, however, it would be much better to preserve than to fall into "the solitary and forlorn condition which must follow upon violence and universal license.") Conceiving men driven into reason by fear, the solution is pseudo-Hobbesian, albeit it is unlikely to work insofar as it falls under Hobbes' own contradictory dictum that, unlike mathematical notions in which truth and interest are not at odds, in regard to any proposition motivated by passion, "nothing is indisputable, because it compareth men and medleth with their right and profit; in which, as oft as reason is against a man, so oft will be a man against reason." More congenial to the developing capitalism was the alternative put into circulation by Adam Smith just before the American Revolution, viz., the collective interest will be served naturally, as if by an Invisible Hand, if each one attends singularly to his own. This seems to be the faith in John Marshall's riposte to Patrick Henry's demand for self-love in the Virginia ratification debates:

> In this country, there is no exclusive stock of interest. The interest of the community is blended and inseparably connected with that of the individual. When he promotes his own good, he promotes that of the community. When we consult the common good, we consult our own. Where he [Henry] desires such checks as these, he will find them abundantly there. They are the best checks.

Engaged in constituting a beneficent *nomos*, society, out of an anti-social *physis*, human nature, the Founders' classicism ran deeper than they were perhaps aware. But rather than relying on the hope that civic virtue would come by itself out of private vice, some argued more effectively for a collective interest based on nationalism and patriotism. As these again thrive best in war and imperial expansion, they rely on external relations of the new republic rather than internal processes. When Alexander Hamilton insisted repeatedly in *The Federalist Papers* that there should be no intermediate bodies between the federal government and individual persons, he was not simply arguing against the sovereign rights of the states. Rather, he allowed that perhaps there was something novel in his demand that the national government "must carry its agency to the persons of the citizens," that it "must be able to address itself immediately to the hopes and fears of individuals; and to attract to its support those passions which have the strongest influence on the human heart." What was novel was the thorough-going nationalism of it. The nation, Hamilton was saying, must insinuate itself in people's lives as an object (subject?) of their fondest sentiments, so that, having thus incorporated the nation in themselves, they find themselves incorporated in the nation.

One might say that in respect of subjectivity, nationalism is a political form of kinship. Like kinship, nationalism involves a mutual predication of being between persons and their country. (This, of course, is its etymology: *nation*, L. 'birth,' 'race.') At about the same time as Hamilton's nationalistic plea, incidentally, Edmund Burke was saying the like about England, although in a monarchial vein. Defending inherited kingship, he said that it gave "to our frame of polity the image of a relation in blood; binding up the constitution of the country with our dearest domestic ties; adapting our fundamental laws into the bosom of our family affections." Hamilton thought to bind the republic with the same sort of attachments. The more the citizens are accustomed to meet with the national authority in the common occurrences of political life, he said,

> The more it is familiarized to their sight and to their feelings, the further it enters those objects which touch the most sensible chords and put in motion the most active springs of the human heart, the greater will be the probability that it will conciliate the respect and attachment of the community....The inference is that the authority of the Union and the affections of the citizens towards it will be strengthened, rather than weakened, by an extension to what are called matters of internal concern....The more it circulates through those channels and currents in which the passions of mankind naturally flow, the less it will require the aid of the violent and perilous expedients of compulsion.

No longer is passion fighting passion. The nation is the passion—the body politics of the body politic.

Moreover, the Founders were disposed to justify a variety of constitutional arrangements by appeals to natural order, whether cosmological or corporeal. Science already provided them with a cosmology appropriate to the self-regulatory republic. As Hofstadter points out, the science boom of the eighteenth century, inspired notably by the rational cosmos of Newton, provided the Founders with a heavenly model of balanced and stable forces in support of the idea that government could be established on the same basis. "Men had found a rational order in the universe." Hofstadter wrote, "and hoped it could be transformed to politics; or, as John Adams put it, that governments could be 'created on the simple principles of nature.'" We have already seen how Adams hopefully transferred the principle of a balanced state of humors in the healthy body to a government that would be stable forever if the political forces could likewise be kept in equilibrium. Indeed, medical treatments in colonial America were still largely dominated by the principle of the restoration of a physiological balance—especially as they were promoted by the influential nightmare-doctor Benjamin Rush. Rush's project was to reduce all manner of diseases to the excessive action of the arterial walls, all of which illness he broadly labeled "fever" and treated by "depleting" or "relaxing" practices, particularly copious bleeding. (If enough blood was taken, the patient would indeed relax, that is, faint.) Even his friend Thomas Jefferson said Rush had done much harm, though persuaded he was doing good. The Englishman William Cobbett deemed Rush's technique "one of those great discoveries that have contributed to the depopulation of the earth."

Well, at least self-interest was recuperating, in Europe as well as America.

The Moral Recuperation of Self-Interest

Considered natural and accorded the positive function of maintaining social equilibrium, the self-interest beating in every human breast was by the end of the eighteenth century well on its way to becoming a good thing—so good that, by the twentieth century, some would claim it was the best thing. Of course, the redemption of Original Sin in the capitalist form of a commendable and calculable self-interest has never been final. On the contrary, it has left us with a scarified contradiction between social morality and individual self-concern (a contradiction also known as "Social Science.") All the same, though it could never quite shake its aura of wickedness, self-pleasing came out of the shadow of its sinful ancestry to assume a moral position nearly 180 degrees removed. The individual's singular attention to his own good turned out to be the basis of society rather than its nemesis—as well as the necessary condition of the greatest wealth of nations.

The transformation began with proponents of the so-called "selfish system" of which Montaigne was a prominent precursor and Hobbes the notorious exemplar. Including luminaries such as Samuel Johnson, Jonathan Swift and Bernard Mandeville together with many lesser lights, the selfish-systematizers had in effect revived the radical sophist notion that natural desires of power and gain were behind all social action, the ostensibly virtuous and benevolent not excepted. "Our virtues are only vices in disguise," read the epigraph of La Rochefoucauld's widely-read *Maxims* (1664). Number 563, for example:

Self-love is the love of oneself and of all things for oneself. It makes men idolize themselves and the tyrants of others, if fortune gives them the means.... Nothing is as impetuous as its desires, nothing so hides its designs, nothing so artful in its conduct. Its suppleness is inexpressible, its transformations surpass the metamorphoses of Ovid, and its refinements those of any chemistry....Such is Self Love! Of which man's life is only a long and great agitation.

Against the Hobbists and their "selfish system" were the many defenders of the "social system" and of the better moral nature of humankind, the third Earl of Shaftesbury prominent among them. But in the long run, given the legitimation of self-interest by the oncoming capitalism, the selfish ideology had the great advantage. Since all would turn out for the material best, one might as well stop complaining about private vice, concluded Mandeville in *The Grumbling Hive*—in a way much like invisible-hand doctrines of times past and to come.

> Then leave Complaints, Fools only strive
> To make a Great and Honest Hive.
> T'enjoy the World's Conveniences,
> Be Famed in War, yet live in Ease,
> Without great Vices, is a vain
> Eutopia seated in the Brain.
> Fraud, Luxury and Pride must live,
> While we the Benefits receive...

Become the happy fault of economy and polity, self-love was being given respect throughout the culture. In the most remarkable turnabout, this evil of ancient memory, rather than destructive of society, was celebrated by famous *philosophes* as the origin thereof. According to Helvétius, Baron d'Holbach, La Méttrie and followers, human need and cupidity, rather than plunging men into anarchy, brought them into society. Instead of enmity, self-interest bred amity: as in Helvétius' memorable dictum, *aimer, c'est avoir besoin*, "to love is to need." People enter into relationships with others for the benefits to themselves, as means to their own ends (which is a kind of Kantian ethical disaster). Scoffs Helvétius: "Every writer who, to give us a good opinion of his own heart, founds the sociability of man on any other principle than that of bodily and habitual wants, deceives weak minds and gives a false idea of morality."

We see now what theory of society was foreshadowed when Aquinas gave an economic declension to Aristotle's determination of man as a political animal. Baron d'Holbach similarly adduced the division of labor, thus the dependence on others in order to further one's own interests, as the reason men congregate in society. Holbach also went on to probe the deeper reason, ravenous desire: "Thus wants, always regenerating, never satisfied, are the principles of life, of activity, the source of health, the basis of society." The anti-Hobbists notwithstanding, the whiff of original sin notwithstanding, here was an all-round theory of culture based on natural egoism—which these days is more popular then ever.

By the twentieth century the worst in us had become the best. Of course for the American revolutionaries, self-interest in the form of each person's pursuit of happiness was already a God-given right. In the logical sequel, possessive individualism was conflated with basic freedom. What St. Augustine had perceived as slavery and indeed divine punishment, man's endless subservience to desires of the flesh, the neo-liberal economists, neo-conservative politicians and most Kansans take to be the bedrock freedom. Freedom is the ability to act in one's own best interest—unhindered notably by government. (The antithesis between state power and self-interest remains, only now that self-interest is the good thing, the least government is the best government.) The complementary idea that self-love is only natural has been reinforced lately by a wave of genetic determinism featuring the "selfish gene" of the sociobiologists and the revived Social Darwinism of the evolutionary psychologists. Moreover, whatever features of culture may have escaped explanation by the supposed natural dispositions of genes to maximize their own advantage can be covered by the "rational choice" theories of economists that similarly account for everything from suicide rates to juvenile delinquency by the prudent allocation of "human capital."

All this "realism" and "naturalism" has been commended as "the disenchantment of the world," although what it really meant was the enchantment of society *by the world*—by the symbolism of body and matter instead of spirit. Not only was society understood as the collective outcome of corporeal wants, but the world was accordingly bespelled by the symbolically-constituted commodity values of gold, pinot noir grapes, oil, filet mignon and pure Fiji water. Here is the construction of nature by particular cultural meanings and practices, whose symbolic qualities are understood however as purely material qualities, whose social sources are attributed rather to bodily desires, and whose arbitrary satisfactions are mystified as universally rational choices.

Other Human Worlds

As enchanted as our universe may still be, it is also still ordered by a distinction of culture and nature that is evident to virtually no one else but ourselves. On the basis of an ethnographic *tour du monde*, Philippe Descola concludes:

> The manner in which the modern Occident represents nature is the one thing in the world the least widely shared. In numerous regions of the planet, humans and non-humans are not conceived as developing in incommensurable worlds according to distinct principles. The environment does not consist of objectivity as an autonomous sphere; plants and animals, rivers and rocks, meteors and seasons, do not exist in the same ontological niche, defined by its lack of humanity.

The positive point is that plants and animals of significance to the people, as also features of the landscape, celestial bodies, meteorological phenomena, even certain artifacts, are beings like themselves: persons with the attributes of humanity—and sometimes the appearance thereof, as in dreams and visions. Like human beings, these other species of persons have souls or are ensouled by spirits, whence their capacities of consciousness, intelligence, intentionality, mobility and emotionality, as well as their ability to communicate meaningfully with each other and with people. This is a cosmos of immanent humanity, as Viveiros de Castro put it, where "relations between human persons and what we call 'nature' takes on the quality of social relations." Or as it is reported of Cree people, for example, "human persons are not set over and against a material context of inert nature but rather are one species of person in a network of reciprocal persons."

Still, the West is not altogether estranged from the Rest by its self-banishment to a soulless universe. We do know at least one non-human person of some significance: God. The Christian God has all the qualities of personhood, even including the ability to assume human form and to die a human death. He also has some angelic persons attending Him. But this Jealous One will not brook any other such gods in his earthly dominions, nor does he inhabit the same sublunar space as his creatures. Christianity (as Judaism before it) distinguished itself from "paganism" by its condemnation of "nature worship," leaving it with a theology of transcendent divinity and the ontology of a purely material world. God having made the world out of nothing, nature was without redeeming spiritual value. "But what is my God?" St. Augustine asks in *The Confessions*, "I put the question to the earth. It answers, 'I am not God,'" and all things on earth declared the same." Never mind that if the earth and all things therein were able to speak to Augustine, his questions about spiritual existence entailed a certain irony.

Developing the same argument against neo-Platonism in *The City of God*, Augustine unwittingly reproves just about all other religions, especially the pantheistic doctrines of Polynesians, the basic concepts of which he repudiates as a blasphemous absurdity. For if the world were the body of God, he says, "who cannot see what impious and irreligious ideas follow, such that whatever one may trample, he must trample a part of God, and in slaying any living creature, a part of God must be slaughtered?" In fact, Augustine accurately describes the ritual predicament of the New Zealand Maori who treads upon the Earth Mother, Papa, injures the god Tāne in cutting down trees, and consumes the ancestor Rongo when eating sweet potatoes. The Maori live in a universe entirely composed of persons, all descended from the primal parents, Earth (Papa) and Heaven (Rangi). In effect, the universe is one big kindred. All the things that surrounded the Maori were their kinsmen, noted the ethnographer Elsdon Best, including trees, birds, insects, fish, stones and "the very elements." On many occasions, Best said, "when felling a tree in the forest, have I been accosted by passing natives with such a remark as...'You are meddling with your ancestor Tāne.'" The implication is that one must observe the appropriate ritual respects.

Even White men were in good genealogical standing among Maori. This would not be true in the personhood system of the Chewong hunter-gatherers of Malaysia. As recorded by Signe Howell, the Chewong figure themselves more closely related to certain non-human persons, including certain artifacts, than they are to Whites and other distant humans. Plants, animals, objects and spirits with whom they share the same habitat and customs they consider "our people," in contrast to Malays, Chinese, Europeans and other aboriginal groups, who are "different people" living by their own laws and languages on the periphery of the Chewong world. Clearly, the schemes of personhood vary. Some peoples make distinctions of degree among other species in the same way that within human groups the very young, the very old and the demented may not be considered complete persons. An elderly Siberian Yukaghir hunter explained to Rane Willerslev that animals, trees and rivers are "people like us" because, having two souls, they move, grow and breathe; whereas stones, skis and food products, while alive, have only one soul, hence are immobile and not the same as human persons—though in practice such differences may break down. Some of these systems of personhood are reminiscent of a of a Chinese system of classification as imagined by Jorge Luis Borghes. The "Ojibway Ontology" described by Irving Hallowell in a foundational article includes in the category of "person:" the sun, moon, kettles, the four winds, pipes, certain shells, the thunderbird, some stones and flint. As documented in the classic ethnography of Waldemar Bogoras, the peoples of eastern Siberia could not be fooled into thinking they saw reality in the shadows on the walls of their caves; they knew that shadows were different tribes who in their own countries lived in cabins and subsisted by hunting.

If all this seems fantastic, it should be remembered that in a universe of reciprocally interacting subjects, even material practice (*praxis*) entails communication with, and knowledge of species-others that is achieved through dreams, myths, spells, incantations, shamanic transformations and their like. As Robin Riddington concluded from long association with the Dunne-za (or Beaver) people of British Columbia, this may involve a different relation between experience and knowledge than we know from common sense and empirical philosophers. As heirs of John Locke, for us knowledge follows from sensory experience of events in a physical world. For the Dunne-za, events follow from the knowledge of them in dreams, myths and the like— a rather more Platonic epistemology. Riddington explains:

The Dunne-za assume…that events can take place only after people have experienced them in myths, dreams and visions Even their concept of person is different from ours. In Dunne-za reality, animals, winds, rocks, and natural forces are "people." Human people are constantly in contact with these nonhuman persons. All persons continually bring the world into being through the myths, dreams and visions they share with one another….The Dunne-za experience myths and dreams as fundamental sources of knowledge…

In this connection, the "magical" power of words and ritual performances may seem less mystical or at least less mystifying when it is realized that they are addressed to persons. As such they are intended to influence these other-than-human persons by rhetorical effects, in the same way as interpersonal dialogue among people moves them to thought and action. For this purpose, a full semiotic repertoire of associations is brought to bear, ranging far afield of the technical dimensions of the activity yet remaining connected to its aims. Praxis becomes poetics, since it is itself persuasive.

Let us concentrate on hunting and hunters' relations to animals, as these are most pertinent to our inquiry into the Western idea of the animal nature of humans, inasmuch as other peoples act on the contrary principle that animals have a human nature. Once again, the contrast is not absolute, since we do accord some human attributes (sometimes even legal status as persons) to some individual animals, mainly domestic pets, mainly dogs. On the other hand, we are speaking here of peoples by whose lights numerous animal species as such, wild and domestic, are persons by nature, living in their own societies of human order, their bodily differences from humans being superficial rather than essential and for that matter transformable into human appearance, even as humans are also known to take animal forms and to live in animal communities. Hence the culture of hunting praxis. Referring to hunter-gatherers in general, Tim Ingold writes: "Hunting itself comes to be regarded not as a technical manipulation of the natural world but as a kind of inter-personal dialogue, integral to the total process of social life, wherein both human and animal persons are consti-tuted with particular identities and purposes." Hunting is a social relationship between humans and animal persons carried on in terms and acts that signify, among other forms of sociality, respect, reciprocity, propitiation, sympathy, taboo, seduction, sacrifice, coercion, recogni-tion, compassion, domination, temptation, surrender and various combinations thereof. Hunting is a cultur-ally-informed, transpecific sociology.

People are thus engaged in transactions with the spirits of animals that correspond to exchanges between human persons and groups. Especially these transactions are likely to resemble exchanges with rela-tives by marriage, insofar as the latter similarly involve fraught negotiations for the transfer of life-powers from one group to another. Levi-Strauss relates a tradition (originally recorded by J. A. Teit) concerning the origin of the wild goat hunt among the Thompson River people of Northwest America, in which the goat prin-cipal is not only human but a brother-in-law of the human hero. The latter is promised he will become a great hunter if he follows certain rules:

> When you kill goats, treat their bodies respectfully, for they are people. Do not shoot the female goats

for they are your wives and will bear your children. Do not kill kids, for they may be your offspring. Only shoot your brothers-in-law, the male goats. Do not be sorry when you kill them, for they do not die but return home. The flesh and skin (the goat part) remain in your possession, but their real selves (the human part) lives just as before, when it was covered with goat's flesh and skin.

In other Amerindian narratives, the hunter becomes a privileged son-in-law of the spirit master of the game species by mating with the master's daughter. Although the neo-Darwinian sciences of our animality, culminating in the current Evolutionary Psychology, would have it that we still suffer genetically from the ferocity that the human species found adaptive in its long history of surviving by the killing of animals, the ethnographic evidence is that hunting is generally more involved with making love than making war.

From about the middle of the last century, expert scientific opinion held that the early human ancestors in Africa, by turning away from the frugivorous diet of the great apes in favor of hunting big game, thereby brought out our depravity and made it our destiny. It was as though the Australopithecine remains had provided paleontological evidence for Original Sin—if in this case by gorging on meat rather than the forbidden fruit. In a single colorful paragraph, Raymond Dart, the first to make a scholarly issue of this hominid horror, attributed the whole "blood-splattered" historical archive from the ancient Egyptians to the atrocities of World War II, together with "early universal cannibalism" and world-wide practices of scalping, head-hunting, body-mutilating and necrophilia, to the

Australopithecines' predaceous habit: "this mark of Cain that separates man dietetically from his anthropoid relatives." Later evidence would show that the great apes were not as frugivorous, nor the Australopithecines as carnivorous as Dart and others had claimed. But even at the time it was evident from contemporary hunter-gatherers that there was no necessary relation between dependence on hunting and violence among people. The much stronger association is between hunting and sexual intercourse, not only as the establishment of affinal relations, but often in the technique itself. Rane Willerslev makes this point at length for the Siberian Yukaghir, and in support cites Rachael-Dolmatoff on the Amazonian Tukano: "hunting is practically a courtship and sexual act;" the verb to hunt translates as "to make love to animals." Good Freudians as we are, we typically interpret dream of success in the chase as sexual conquests. Hunting people typically interpret dreams of sexual conquests as signs of future success in the chase— knowledge coming before experience.

It follows, as a condition of such transpecific communication, that animals are human under the skin. Their bodily forms are superficial—and often discardable to reveal their underlying humanity, as happens in people's dreams. Just as different human groups are distinguished by their dress and ornamentation—which may well consist of furs or feathers—so may animal bodies be the clothing, or perhaps the disguise, of the species' personhood. Also implied by the transpecific communication is that the animals have the same culture as the people. Accounts from many Native Americans testify that animals in their own countries live in houses, have chiefs, marry, hold ceremonies and in general practice the same customs as the people do. Moreover, from their own vantage point the animals see themselves as human; whereas, they see humans as spirits or animal species, often as predators. This "perspectivism," as so named and brilliantly analyzed by Viveiros de Castro, is a function of the bodily differences of species. All species experience the same things, yet the things they are thus seeing, the objective referents, vary. The jaguar of the South American forests sees manioc beer where humans see blood; what humans see as a muddy river bank, tapirs see as a ceremonial house, etc. What Chewong of Malaysia perceive as faeces, their dogs see as bananas— not to get upset, then.

Not to wonder either at the ethnographic reports from New Guinea or the Americas that animals were human in origin. Animals are descended from humans rather than the other way around. "While our folk anthropology," writes Viveiros de Castro,

> holds that humans have an original animal nature which must be coped with by culture—having been wholly animals, we remain animals at bottom— Amerindian thought likewise holds that having been human, animals must still be human, albeit in a non-evident way.

It is as if the human and the animal as we know them, and indeed *nomos* and *physis*, had traded places. For in the common opinion of mankind, what we call "natural" is superficial and conditional, as in the changeable appearance of animals whose humanity rather is their essential condition. Humanity is the universal, nature is the particular. Humanity is the original state, from which the natural forms were produced and differentiated.

One has to ask, if man really has a pre-social, anti-social animal disposition, how has it happened that so many peoples remained unaware of it and lived to relate their ignorance? Many of them have no concept of animality whatsoever, let alone of the bestiality supposed to be lurking in our genes, our bodies and our culture. Amazing that, living in such close relations with so-called "nature," these peoples have neither recognized their inherent animality nor known the necessity of coming to cultural terms with it.

Now is the Whimper of Our Self-Contempt

For that matter, not even wild animals are wild animals. I mean they are not the savage beasts men are supposed to be by nature, driven by their insatiable appetites to sow war and disorder among their own kind. Now is the whimper of our self-contempt: *homo homini lupus*, "man is a wolf to man," the formula of dark human instincts adopted by Freud after the popular characterization of Hobbism, based in turn on an aphorism authored by Plautus in the second century BC. (Freud did wonder, however, how beasts managed to deal with such a fundamental menace to the species.) What a slander of the gregarious wolf-pack with its many techniques of deference, intimacy and cooperation, whence its enduring order. After all we are speaking of the ancestor of "man's best friend." Nor are the great ape relatives of humanity bent on "a perpetual and restless desire pursuit of power after power that ceaseth only in death" and, in consequence, a "war of each against all." There is nothing in nature as perverse as our idea of human nature. It is a figment of our cultural imagination.

Freud's modern version of human bestiality in *Civilization and Its Discontents* echoes the many centuries of the Western hatred of self. Besides Hobbes or Augustine, do you not hear Thucydides' ghost?

> *Homo homini lupus*; who has the courage to dispute it in the face of all the evidence in his own life and history?...In circumstances that favor it, when those forces in the mind that ordinarily inhibit it cease to operate, it also manifests itself spontaneously and reveals men as savage beasts to whom the thought of

> sparing their own kind is alien....The existence of this tendency to aggression which we can detect in ourselves and rightly presume to be present in others is the factor that disturbs our relations with our neighbors and makes it necessary for culture to institute its high demands. Civilized society is perpetually menaced with disintegration through this primary hostility of men towards one another....Culture has to call up every possible reinforcement in order to erect barriers against the aggressive instincts of men and hold their manifestations in check by reaction-formations in men's minds.

For Freud, "nothing is so completely at variance with the original human nature" as "the ideal command to love one's neighbor."

In Freudian psychoanalysis, the socialization of the child is a repetition of the collective social history of the repression or sublimation of this malignant original nature. The longstanding alternative of childhood innocence, a reflex of the subdominant ideology of good nature/bad culture, could have no credence for Freud. He would have endorsed Augustine's observation (from *The Confessions*) that "if babes are innocent, it is not for lack of will to do harm, but for lack of strength." Freudian theory, in which the primitive anti-social instincts of the child—specifically, libidinal and aggressive instincts—are put down by a superego representing the role of the father and more largely the culture, thus takes the specific Augustinian or Hobbesian form of the sovereign domination of man's anarchic impulses. (Though it could be argued that the first regulation of the child's all-out search for pleasure by the "reality principle" is more like a political order of off-setting powers, insofar as it involves the frustration of infantile desires by others attending rather to their own good. In any case, the infant's grasping of "reality" through experiences of pleasure and pain is a virtual replication of Hobbes' empiricist epistemology in the opening chapters of *Leviathan*.) So again, what should we make of the considerable ethnographic evidence to the contrary: that all round the world, other peoples know no such idea of children as innate monsters and no such necessity of domesticating their bestial instincts.

"The Hagen view of the person does not require that a child be trained into social adulthood from some pre-social state, nor postulate that each of us repeats the original domestication of humanity in the need to deal with elements of a precultural nature." Society, Marilyn Strathern goes on to say, "is not a set of controls over and against the individual; human achievements do not culminate in culture." In fact, few societies known to anthropology, besides our own, make the domestication of infants' inherent anti-social dispositions the issue of their socialization. On the contrary, the average common opinion of mankind is that sociality is the normal human condition. I am tempted to say that sociality is generally considered "innate," except that the people do not regard themselves as composed of a biological substratum—certainly not an animal substratum—on or against which culture is constructed. Clearly this would be a biological fallacy for those who know themselves as reincarnations of deceased relatives, as is the common fact of infant life in West Africa, Northern North American and Northern Eurasia. Willersev observes of Yukaghir that in their world "there is no such thing as a child," for infants are understood to have the skills, knowledge, temperament and attributes of the dead kinsmen who ensoul them. Many of these characteristics are forgotten when the child acquires language, and only gradually recuperated through his or her lifetime. In a work titled *The Afterlife is Where We Come From*, Alma Gottlieb describes the functionally similar idea of the Beng people of Côte d'Ivoire: that the child only gradually manifests the persona of the kinsman it incarnates because the other dead try to retain the latter in their midst.

The more common belief is simply that the infant is not yet a full person—although not because he or she is born an anti-person. This incompleteness is a question of the maturity of child's mind or soul rather than the regulation of bodily impulses. Personhood is gradually achieved through social interactions, especially those involving reciprocity and interdependence, for these comprise and teach the child's social identities. Fijian children have "watery souls" (*yalo wai*) until they understand and practice the obligations of kinship and chiefship (Anne Becker, Christina Toren). Children of Ifalik island in Micronesia are "mindless" (*bush*) until five or six, when they have acquired sufficient "intelligence" (*reply*) to give them a moral sense (Catherine Lutz). Small children in Java are "not yet Javanese"(*ndurung djawa*), by contrast to the "already Javanese" (*sampun djawa*), that is, the normal adult capable of practicing the society's elaborate etiquette and delicate aesthetic and "responsive to the subtle promptings of the divine residing in the stillness of each individual's inward-turning consciousness" (Clifford Geertz). Childhood for Aymara people of Highland Bolivia is a progression from imperfect to perfected humanity, marked by the assumption of social obligations, yet notably without "the punitive element in the concept of *repression* that we use to express the process by which a baby is socialized" (Olivia Harris). For the Mambai of Timor, infants, like Portuguese, have as yet undifferentiated "whole" or "full" hearts, a closure to the world that implies a sort of unawareness or stupor (Elizabeth Traube). The Chewong of Malaysia say that the soul of the child is not fully developed, not until he or she can carry out adult responsibilities as signified by marriage (Signe Howell). Just so in Hagen again, the child grows into maturity "through appreciation of what social relationships with others involve." The infant "is certainly not rømi ['wild']," and is less trained than nurtured to personhood (Strathern). Speaking more generally of Melanesian concepts of sociability, Strathern observes that they do not entail the supposition of a society that lies over and above the individual as a set of forces for controlling the latter's resistance. "The imagined problems of social existence are not those of an exteriorized set of norms, values, or rules that must be constantly propped up and sustained against realities that constantly appear to subvert them."

By comparison with our orthodox views of early childhood—popular or scientific—societies around the world oppose a certain culturalism to our biologism. For them, infants are humanity-in-becoming; for us, animality-to-be-overcome. Most peoples surely do not think the child as double, half angel and half beast. Rather, children are born human, whether incompletely so or fully so by incarnation. Their maturation consists of the acquisition of the mental capacity to assume proper social relationships. Implied is the recognition that human life, including the expression of faculties and dispositions, is meaningfully constituted—in the cultural forms, moreover, of a given society. But where the Rest are attending the progression of mind, the West is worrying about the expression of body. Here the behavior of the infant is largely figured in the organic terms of "need" and "appetite," even as the child's egoism is confirmed by treating these as "demands." Perhaps we would not view babes as self-centered creatures of desire were we not already committed egoists ourselves. Thank Freud for another relevant concept: projection.

In the received Western folklore, the "savage" (them) is to the "civilized" (us) as nature to culture and body to mind. Yet in anthropological fact, nature and body are the ground of the human condition for us; for them, it is culture and mind. To adapt a phrase penned by Lévi-Strauss in reference to an analogous context, who then does more credit to the human race?

Culture is the Human Nature

Who, then, are the realists? The realists, I believe, are the aforementioned peoples who take culture as the original state of human existence and the biological species as secondary and conditional. For in a critical sense, they are right, and the paleontological record of hominid evolution will support them—as so again does Geertz who brilliantly drew out the anthropological implications. Culture is older than *Homo sapiens*, many times older, and culture was a fundamental condition of the species' biological development. Evidence of culture in the human line goes back about three million years; whereas the current human form is but a few hundred thousand years old. Or else, to follow the influential human biologist Richard Klein, anatomically modern man is only 50,000 years old and flourished particularly in the late Stone Age (Upper Paleolithic), which would make culture sixty times older than the species as we know us. (However, Klein is inclined to systematically depreciate the cultural and corporeal achievements of earlier hominids in the interest of positing a radical, biologically-based cultural advance in the Upper Paleolithic.) The critical point is that for some three million years humans evolved biologically under cultural selection. We have been fashioned body and soul for a cultural existence.

A parenthesis here. Speaking of body and soul, one ought to note a parallel concept of their evolution among the ancients of the Western tradition. Perhaps Plato was intentionally undermining certain sophists when he claimed that soul, as the only entity capable of self-movement, is older than body, which it moves and fashions. Moreover, as soul is realized in art, law and the like, this is also to say that *nomos* is older than and the source of *physis*. So he argued in the *Laws*, *Timaeus*, *Phaedo* and elsewhere. In the *Laws* (10.896a-b) he says that body, being "secondary and derivative" is subject to soul, which means that "moods and habits of mind, wishes, calculations, and true judgments, purposes and memories, will all be prior to physical lengths, breadths and depths." Thus culture before nature:

> And so judgment and foresight, wisdom, art and law, must be prior to hard and soft, heavy and light. Aye and the grand primal works and deeds, for the very reason they are primal, will prove to be those of art; those of nature and nature herself—wrongly so called—will be secondary and derivative from art and mind (10.892b).

Why is nature wrongly so called? Because soul/culture came first, hence it is really soul "which is the most eminently *natural*" (*Laws* 892b-c). Or phrasing the implication in current anthropological terms: culture is the human nature. End parenthesis.

No ape can tell the difference between holy water and distilled water, Leslie White used to say, because there is no difference chemically. Yet the meaningful difference makes all the difference for how people value and use holy water; even as, unlike apes, whether or not they are thirsty makes no difference in such regard. That was my brief lesson on what means "symbol" and what means "culture." Regarding the implications for human nature, leading a life according to culture means having the ability and knowing the necessity of achieving our bodily inclinations symbolically, that is, according to meaningful determinations of ourselves and the objects of our existence. This symbolic encompassment of the body, of its needs and drives, was the significant effect of the long history of cultural selection out of which emerged *Homo sapiens*.

Respectable biological opinion now has it that the human brain is a social organ: that it evolved in the Pleistocene under the "pressure" of maintaining a relatively extensive, complex and solidary set of social relationships—which in all probability included kinds of non-human persons. Symbolic capacity was a necessary condition of this social capacity. The "pressure" was to become a cultural animal; or more exactly, to culturalize our animality. Not that we are or ever were "blank slates," lacking any biological imperatives; only that what was uniquely selected for in the genus *Homo* was the inscription of these imperatives in and as variable forms of meaning, hence the ability to realize them in the untold ways that archaeology, history and ethnography have demonstrated. Nor am I denying the currently popular theory of co-evolution: the notion that culture and biological developments reciprocally gave impetus to each other. But that does not mean that the effect was an equal valence of these as "factors" in human social existence. On the contrary, there had to be an inverse relation between the variety and complexity of cultural patterns and the specificity of biological dispositions. In the co-evolution, the development of culture would have to be complemented by the deprogramming of genetic imperatives or what used to be called instinctual behaviors. The effect was the organization of biological functions in various cultural forms, such that the expression of biological necessities depended on meaningful logics.

We have the equipment to live a thousand different lives, as Clifford Geertz observed, although we end up living only one. This is only possible on the condition that biological needs and drives do not specify the particular means of their realization. Biology becomes a determined determinant.

So again, who are the realists? Would it not be the Fijians who say that young children have "watery souls," meaning that they are not full human beings until they demonstrate the mastery of Fijian custom? We have seen that peoples round the planet have some such similar idea. The idea is that human nature is a *becoming*, based on the capacity to comprehend and enact the appropriate cultural scheme: a *becoming*, rather than an always-already being. Or as Kenneth Bock has phrased it, the misplaced concreteness of human nature as an *entity* is a basic aspect of our mythology of it. We speak of determinate cultural practices as somehow inscribed in the germ plasm: most recently in the genes, before that the instincts and before that in the semen. Still, the issue is not whether human nature is basically this or that, good or bad. The issue is biologism itself. The many critics of Montaigne, Hobbes, Mandeville & Co., by attacking innate egoism on grounds of man's natural goodness or natural sociability, remained within the same sclerotic framework of a corporeal determination of cultural forms. As Bock also points out, a true alternative begins in the Renaissance with philosophical moves that would liberate humankind from the predetermined evil of Original Sin.

In this connection, Bock singles out Pico della Mirandola's *Oration on the Dignity of Man*, a classic text of Renaissance self-fashioning. Having created the world, God then wanted to make a creature who could appreciate its beauty and grandeur; but when He thus went to make man, there was no form or space left over for such a work. So, wrote Pico, since God could give man nothing wholly his own, He decided to make him a "creature of indeterminate image," placed at the center of the world where he could "have a share in the particular endowment of every other creature." Says God to Adam:

> The nature of all other creatures is defined and restricted within laws which we have laid down; you, by contrast, impeded by no such restrictions, may, by your own free will, to whose custody We have assigned you, trace for yourself the lineaments of your own nature....We have made you a creature neither of heaven nor of earth, neither mortal nor immortal, in order that you may, as the free and proud shaper of your own being, fashion yourself in the form you prefer. It will be in your power to descend to the lower, brutal forms of life; you will be able, through your own decision, to rise again to the superior orders whose life is divine.

Besides humans' inherent ability to lead a thousand different lives, one is reminded of the great arc of temperamental possibilities in Ruth Benedict's *Patterns of Culture*, of which each culture selectively exploits but a limited segment.

When moral philosophers of the Scottish Enlightenment, Adam Ferguson particularly, took up the cause of human will against predetermined sin or instinct, they added a social dimension that set the course to an anthropological understanding of human nature as a culturally-informed becoming. Ferguson went beyond the usual defense of free will on the grounds that moral agency would be meaningless if we cannot not sin. For Ferguson, man was truly a social animal, but precisely in the sense that his nature was formed in society rather than innately pre-posed to it or responsible for it. There is no such pre-social individual, no such thing as a human being existing before or apart from society. Humans are constituted, for better or for worse, within society, and variously so in different societies. In society they are born, and there they remain, said Ferguson (after Montesquieu), capable of all the sentiments on which diverse peoples fashion their mode of life. And it is from the necessary social formation of humanity that Ferguson concludes in a golden passage:

> If we are asked therefore, where is the state of nature to be found? We may answer, It is here; and it matters not whether we are understood to speak in the island of Great Britain, at the Cape of Good Hope, or in the Straits of Magellan.

Similarly for Marx, the "human essence" exists in and as social relationships, not in some poor bugger squatting outside the universe. Humans individualize themselves only in the context of society, if in a certain egoistic way in the European context—which thus gave rise to the economists' fantasies ("Robinsonades") of constituting their science from the supposed dispositions of a single isolated adult male. Nor did Marx indulge in deriving social formations from innate inclinations, although one could certainly read the other way around: from bourgeois society to the mythical Hobbesian war of each against all. Born neither good nor bad, human beings make themselves in social activity as it unfolds in given historical circumstances. One might suppose that Marx's knowledge of colonized others contributed to this anthropology. In any event, with the important proviso that "given cultural orders" replace the "given historical circumstances" in Marx's formulation, or in other words that the *praxis* by which people make themselves is culturally informed, this understanding of the human condition became an ethnographic commonplace.

The state of nature: "it is here." For culture is the human nature. When the Javanese say, "To be human is to be Javanese," Geertz, who reports it, says they are right, in the sense that "there is no such thing as human nature independent of culture." Or again, Margaret Mead in *Growing Up in New Guinea*, responding to the Rousseauean views of educators who would remove the distortions of human nature imposed on children by wrong-minded adults:

> It is, however, a more tenable attitude to regard human nature as the rawest, most undifferentiated of raw material, which will have no form worthy of recognition unless it is shaped and formed by cultural tradition.

One might have better said that people form themselves within a given cultural tradition, but the point remains that the tradition thus informs their modes of bodily needs and satisfactions.

Regarding sex, for example, what is most pertinent to the relations between biology and culture is not that all cultures have sex, but that all sex has culture. Sexual desires are variously expressed and repressed according to local determinations of appropriate partners, occasions, times, places and bodily practices. We sublimate our generic sexuality in all kinds of ways—including its transcendence in favor of the higher values of celibacy, which also proves that in symbolic regimes there are more compelling ways of achieving immortality than the inscrutable mystique of the "selfish gene." After all, immortality is a thoroughly symbolic phenomenon—what else could it be? (In *The Theory of Moral Sentiments*, Adam Smith observes that men have been known to voluntarily throw away lives to acquire after death a renown which they could no longer enjoy, being content to anticipate in the imagination the fame it would bring them.) Likewise, sexuality is realized in various meaningfully-ordered forms. Consider that some Western people even do it by telephone—lest you think that hunting is a bizarre way of making love. Or for another example of conceptual manipulation (pun intended), there is Bill Clinton's, "I did not have sexual relations with that woman."

As it is for sex, so for other inherent needs, drives or dispositions: nutritional, aggressive, sociable, compassionate—whatever they are, they come under symbolic definition and thus cultural order. In the occurrence, aggression or domination may take the behavioral form of, say, the New Yorker's response to, "Have a nice day"—"DON'T TELL ME WHAT TO DO!" We war on the playing fields of Eton, give battle with swear words and insults, dominate with gifts that cannot be reciprocated or write scathing book reviews of academic adversaries. Eskimo say gifts make slaves, like whips make dogs. But to think that, or to think our proverbial opposite, that gifts make friends—a saying that like the Eskimos' goes against the grain of the prevailing economy—requires that we are born with "watery souls," waiting to manifest our humanity for better or worse in the meaningful experiences of a particular way of life. Not, however, as in our ancient philosophies and modern sciences, that we are condemned by an irresistible human nature to look to our own advantage at the cost of whomever it may concern and thus menace our own social existence.

It's all been a huge mistake. My modest conclusion is that Western civilization has been constructed on a perverse and mistaken idea of human nature. Sorry, beg your pardon; it was all a mistake. It is probably true, however, that this perverse idea of human nature endangers our existence. ∎

Also available from Prickly Paradigm Press:

continued